Do What You Got to Do

Julia Graziano

978-1-965552-00-1 (Paperback)

BOOKWRIGHTS
HOUSE

admin@bookwrightshouse.com
12211 W Washington Blvd.
Suite 110, Los Angeles CA 90066

1

IN THE END, IT didn't matter what color black she wore. Actually she really didn't have to wear black at all. At least that was the way it was these days. No one wore black at funerals anymore, but she was brought up in a family that believed it showed love and respect for the person who died. It wasn't because they thought the newly departed could see what they were wearing; it was more of a reminder to themselves and others who attended that there was now a black space in their lives where before it was filled with color, the color of the person who lay before them. Some were red like fire and burned with passion; some yellow, always the optimist; or green like the trees that grew steady and strong; and brown like the earth and could balance everything on their shoulders. They were different colors to different people, but now the color was gone. Each person felt their own loss, and just by looking at them, you couldn't tell who suffered more—those who sat quietly, looking around the room at the wall of flowers, or those that let a single tear roll down their face and tried catching it with their tongue, or those who cried openly with loud sobs and tears flowing heavily, with their noses red from constant wiping. No, you couldn't tell. The only thing you we're sure of was that a person who meant something to you in life was gone.

2

SHE WAS WEARING BLACK the first time she meet JR. She was wearing a black lace bra and panties, blouse, and skirt. She and a few friends had gone to the local bar just before her last semester in college. Devon decided to take an extra year so she could take some accounting courses. If she planned on having her own business, she wanted to know how to keep the books. Besides, her father was terrible at it for the lodge and was always asking her to fix things before the accountant got them. Devon's friend Sarah had finished her hairdressing course and was already working in a shop in town. She said she loved it, but Devon had her doubts. She wouldn't be surprised if she and the loser boyfriend she had took off with got married. Devon knew it would break her parents' heart if she did, but Sarah wasn't thinking about anything or anyone. The minute she hooked up with this guy, it was like he had complete control of her. Anything he said was all right with Sarah. Devon tried to talk to her about the control he had on her, but Sarah snapped at her; something she had never done in all the years they were friends. Devon decided to let Sarah make her own choices, and hopefully she wouldn't be hurt too badly when he walked out on her like Devon knew he would.

The gang was having fun playing pool, shooting darts, and filling the jukebox with money. The guys were drinking beer and were getting to silly for Devon. She finally decided she had had enough of their sophomoric behavior and went to sit at the bar. She just had a birthday, and now she was twenty-one and legal in New York. Devon ordered a scotch and water. She never really liked beer like the others. She sat quietly and sipped her drink. As she brought her glass up to her mouth, her eyes looked across the bar and met his eyes staring back at her. She recognized JR but knew he probably didn't recognize her. She had seen him around town from time to time but never spoke to him since that day when she was eight. Devon remembered that day with a smile. JR must have thought the smile was an invitation to get closer. He left his barstool and made his way around toward her. The years hadn't been too bad for JR. At thirty-six, he looked strong and tan. Working outdoors all summer hadn't weathered his face yet. It was smooth, and the leftover tan from the summer gave him a healthy glow. He was tall, maybe six feet two, and had a long, slender, but muscular body. Devon's heart started to race, but she drew in a long breath and quickly regained her composure. The last thing she wanted was for him to see how nervous she was. She looked back across the bar, pretending not to notice when he sat down next to her. JR was always quiet but projected an air of authority wherever he went. Devon knew the Ledger name called for respect, and it was given. He sat for a while then spoke to her.

"Aren't you Devon Taylor?" he asked.

"Yes," she answered.

"Father still run the lodge?"

"Yes," she answered again not bothering to look at him.

"Can you say anything besides yes?" he asked.

"Yes, I can," Devon answered.

"Well, it's pretty damn difficult to keep up a conversation if all you're going to say is yes," he replied.

"I didn't know we were having a conversation," answered Devon.

"Well, I'm trying to," he said.

"And what would you like to converse about?" Devon said, finally turning to look at him.

"I don't know. The weather, what you've been doing, how your parents are, how my parents are, anything just so we're talking," he said with a touch of anger in his voice.

"All right, the weather is nice for this time of year. Not too cold, but I would like to see some more snow. My parents are enjoying good health, and from the last article in the paper, you're parents just returned from a vacation abroad, so I'm assuming they are enjoying good health also. Was there anything else?"

"Yes, goddamn it, my parents are fine indeed," he said in a huff.

"If I knew you were so stuck-up, I wouldn't have bothered you."

"I'm not stuck-up. I'm just cautious about who I start a conversation with in a bar," said Devon.

"Well, you know who I am, don't you?"

"Everyone knows who you are, JR," she replied.

"So what's the damn problem?" he said, flustered. Just the way Devon wanted him.

"There's no problem, JR. It's just a little too noisy in here."

"Well, that problem can be easily rectified. Grab your coat, and we'll get out of here," he said. "Wait for me by the door. I have to grab my jacket and pay the bill." Devon walked over to the pool table where she had hung up her coat and said good night to those that were left. A few of the guys begged her to come back and play with them, but she said it was late, and she had to be up early, which really was not a lie. She had to redo the floral arrangement in the lobby of the lodge, and she liked to work before people started getting up for breakfast and began to crowd around her, watching as she arranged the flowers. She retrieved her coat and put it on and went to wait by the door for JR. When he arrived, he asked her if there was some place she would like to go. She really hadn't thought that far ahead, so just told him to choose. He asked if she had her own car, and she told him she did. He told her to follow him in her car so it wouldn't be left at the bar. It made sense to Devon, so she agreed. She had no idea where they were going until he turned and took the road toward his house. He pulled into the driveway of the bungalow he was living in; the one he lived in when he was married. He and his wife divorced a year ago, and she was given a substantial settlement with which she bought a house nearer to the city, plus she was receiving monthly support payments because of their daughter; the daughter that JR rarely saw, partially because of the difficulty his wife always made when he tried to see her and because he didn't have much patience for a child, even his child. It was amazing what you could learn just listening to the gossip around the lodge or the flower shop. Devon hated gossip but couldn't help listening when any of the Ledgers were mentioned.

JR opened her car door and told her to be careful. The driveway was sometimes slippery. She told him she was fine, so he turned and went to unlock the door to the bungalow. He stood aside while Devon went in, then closed the door, walked in, and turned on some lights. He told her to come into the living room, and he would start a fire to take the chill off. She followed and watched as he put a match to the wood that was already loaded with kindling and paper. He must keep it ready to go at a moment's notice in case he brought someone home. She removed her coat and laid it on the wingback chair to the right of the fireplace. She watched as the paper burned hot enough to start the kindling and finally the split wooden logs. She loved the way a fire sounded; the crackles and pops as the wood burned. The fireplace at the lodge was nearly three times as large, with low sofas so a lot of people could sit near it to warm up after a day outside. Devon was momentarily lost in the fire and didn't hear JR ask what she would like to drink.

"I'm sorry. I love watching a fire dance to the music it plays for itself," she said.

"I never heard it put that way, but I guess you're right. It does sound a little like music. Strange music but music it is. Now how about that drink?" Devon said she would have a little scotch and water if he had it. He did and brought it to her where she sat on the sofa facing the fire.

"How does it feel to be living here single?" she asked him.

"'Bout the same way it did when I was married," he answered.

"My wife was a bitch, and I tried not to be home too often. Just came home to sleep and sometimes not even then."

"I'm sorry you had a difficult marriage," said Devon.

"Yeah, well, it was my own damn fault. Can't blame anyone else. She was a conniving bitch, and I should have known she would get pregnant on purpose. She made such a stink around town that I had to marry her," he said sadly.

"Do you miss your daughter?" asked Devon.

"Not really, to be honest. I never wanted kids. Don't have the patience for them." His honesty surprised her.

Devon thought back to the day she first met JR. She was eight, and he was twenty-three. She and her best friend, Sarah McConnell, were cutting through the woods on their way back to the dairy farm that Sarah's father managed for JR's father. His family owned most of the land that stretched from the Catskill Mountains to the Hudson River, much the same way the Livingstons owned land on the other side of the river in the Clermont Region. Russell's family had sold off much of the land over the years, but they still owned a considerable amount. The land was divided into three prominent areas—the dairy farm, the fruit farm, and the land that was used primarily for the Hunt Club. The Ledgers had held the title of Master of the Hounds for many years, and Russell Sr. prided himself on the breeding and training of his hounds. The horse barns and the breeding grounds for the hounds were the closest to the main house, which was a considerable distance from the rest of the property. Russell Sr. had very little to do with the dairy farm or the fruit farm, instead employing managers for them. Now, his time was taken over completely to his horses and dogs, both of which JR had an extreme distaste for, nor did he like the cows or the fruit farm but was made to choose one to work at, and so he chose the fruit farm. That was where Devon and Sarah first saw him. They were trying to hide behind the trees at the end of the cow pasture, having just come from the little stream that they liked to play in. There he was, riding the tractor, cutting the long weeds under the fruit trees. He didn't have a shirt on; his body was glistening with sweat as he drove the tractor under the trees. The girls giggled each time the tractor got a little closer to them. Sarah said he was the most handsome boy she ever saw. Her only comparison being the boys in her school and most of them were horrible to her, saying she always smelled of cow manure. Devon wasn't sure how she felt about him.

JR was the name everyone called him; he said he had outgrown being called Junior and wanted to be called JR. His mother stilled called him Junior, but she was the only one that he let get away with it. He became annoyed with anyone who called him anything other than JR and let them know it. Most took him seriously. He had a short fuse, and with the Ledger name, he expected to get what he wanted and usually did. Devon and Sarah had heard he got a girl pregnant when he was in school, but no one ever spoke about it; and whenever his name was brought up by Sarah in her house, her father came down on her hard and told her that she was never to go near him and made it very clear that if she was ever caught bothering him, she would be punished. And that was why the girls stayed hidden in the bushes. They thought they would be safe there but soon learned they weren't. Everywhere JR went, he had a big, old hound with him who liked to lie asleep under a tree until JR headed back to the house; then he would run after him, knowing work was done for the day, and that usually meant dinnertime for him. The rustling of the bushes caught the old hound's attention, and he immediately took off in their direction. The girls didn't know if they should run or not. If they ran, they knew the dog would chase them down; but if they stayed, they risked being caught, and most likely, their parents would be told, and they would be in more trouble. Sarah decided to run, but Devon chose not to. Either way she thought they were in trouble, so why bother running. As Sarah started to run, Devon stepped out from behind the bushes into the open field. JR took no notice until the hound started baying. He watched the hound as he ran and saw the little girl looking back at him. He could care less who she was, but he was concerned that the dog might hurt her. He called to the dog, "Beaver, stop," but the dog continued. When he reached Devon, he had gained enough speed and launched himself at her, knocking her to the ground. JR got to them as Devon was getting up, seemingly unafraid of the dog.

"Beaver, come here, boy," he said as he reached her. The dog looked at him then at Devon and sat down alongside her.

looked at him then at Devon and sat down alongside her. "Are you hurt?" he asked. "You kids know you shouldn't be around here. Where's that other little one who lives at the farm? Her dad won't be happy if he catches her here."

"She ran when she saw the dog coming. She's afraid of dogs. I'm not, but he did scratch my leg," answered Devon.

"Well, let's have a look," said JR as Devon turned around.

"Yeah, he got you pretty good. You're bleeding," he said.

"It's nothing. I've had worse," answered Devon, trying to act bravely.

"Let's see if we can stop some of the bleeding," said JR as he took out his handkerchief and placed it over the scratch. "Here, hold this on there tight." Devon did as she was told and held it tightly over the scratch. It burned but she didn't say anything.

"I guess you're not afraid of Beaver, and he seems to like you. Not many people old Beaver really likes," he said.

"That's a funny name for a dog," said Devon.

"Yeah, well, he isn't just any dog. Dad raised him to run after the fox, but old Beaver here had other ideas. He preferred chasing the beavers down by the creek because he loves the water, so that's how he got his name," replied JR. "So what do they call you?"

"I'm Devon Taylor, and I'm not afraid of him. And when I grow up, I'm going to have my very own dogs." Devon stood straight with her arms crossed in front of her, looking at him defiantly.

"Well, Devon Taylor, I'm sure you will. Now I think it best if you went on home."

"I can't," she answered. "I'm staying with Sarah at the farm until tomorrow because my parents went to New York City to get some new furniture for the lodge."

"Your parents own the Taylor Lodge up on the mountain?" he asked.

"Yup," said Devon nodding her head.

"That's a nice place you got up there. Get lots of people in the summer?"

"Yeah, we do. The winter too. People come up to ski. I don't like to ski. I always fall down."

"Well, you keep at it. I'm sure you'll do all right. Now head off to the farm and find your friend. She's probably waiting for you up there on the trail somewhere, and Beaver, you come with me." JR turned and walked away with the dog, obviously torn between following Devon, who he knew was kind, and the man who gave him his food at the end of the day. The food won out. Sarah was waiting for Devon not far from the house.

"Why didn't you run with me?" she asked.

"What for? I figured we would be in trouble either way, and besides, I wanted to see the dog," said Devon. "He didn't mean it, but he scratched me on the back of my leg, see. JR gave me this to put on it to stop the bleeding."

"You have to hide the handkerchief. If my father sees it, he'll know we were where we're not supposed to be, and we'll get grounded," cried Sarah.

"How will he know that it isn't mine? I could have a handkerchief like this. Lots of people do," said Devon.

"No, he'll know. It's got his initials on it. Now stuff it in your pocket and hide it in your overnight bag when we get in the house, please," begged Sarah.

"Okay, scaredy-pants," said Devon.

The girls got back to the house just in time for dinner. Pretending she needed to wash up, Devon ran up to her room to hide the handkerchief. She put it in her bag and said to herself that she would never ever wash it because JR gave it to her. This was her first crush.

3

"You know we've met before, don't you?" said Devon.

"No, I think I would have remembered you if I had," answered JR. "When did we meet?"

"I was eight and playing with my friend Sarah McConnell from the dairy farm. We were playing in the woods near where you were mowing under the fruit trees, and Sarah started to run when she saw your dog, but I stepped out, and he ran toward me and knocked me down, scratching my leg. You gave me a handkerchief to stop the bleeding. I remember his name too. It was Beaver," said Devon.

"Well, I'll be. I do remember that now. I remember you were trying to act like you weren't scared, and you did a good job at it too. I'll give you that," he replied.

"I wasn't scared, just startled when he knocked me down. I still have the scar to prove it," said Devon.

"I'd sure like to see that," he said jokingly. Devon stood up and undid the button and the zipper on her skirt and let it fall to the floor. JR just stood there, looking at her. She was gorgeous, with long, slender legs; the kind that went all the way up, and the rest of the body wasn't bad either. He was so taken by surprise when she let her skirt fall. He was at a loss for words. It was Devon who finally spoke.

"Don't you want to see the scar?" JR was not sure what to do. Was this a serious invitation, or was she just playing a game?

"I'll tell you now that if I come over there, it won't be just the scar I'll be wanting to see, so be sure of what you're saying," he said.

"I'm sure," she replied. JR bent down as she turned around and pointed to the back of her leg where the scar was. JR ran his finger over it and said thankfully that it wasn't so bad. Then he leaned forward and kissed it.

"There, all better. A little late, but better late than never," he said jokingly. "You have some great legs. I'm guessing the rest of the body is just as beautiful. I'd sure like to see it."

"Would you?" replied Devon.

"Why don't we go to the bedroom and you can show me," he said as he ran his hands up her body.

"Is that where you take all your women?"

"I do. Have something else in mind?" he said surprisingly.

"What about here?" she said. "Push the sofa back and put the quilt here on the floor." JR looked at her, and when she didn't say anything else, he did what she said. He pushed the sofa out of the way and folded the large quilt and placed it between the sofa and the fireplace.

"This what you had in mind?" he said.

"It will do," said Devon as she began to unbutton her blouse. JR jumped to assist her. Once her blouse was off, she stood there in her black lace bra and black bikini panties.

"Wow, great legs, great body, beautiful face, and still trying to be brave. You got it all, I'll say that for you," said JR.

"Need help with your shirt?" said Devon as she moved closer to him.

"I guess I could use a hand," he said. Devon pulled his shirt out of his pants, unbuttoned the first button, then took each side of the shirt in her hands, and tore the rest off in one swift motion.

"Hey, that was my best shirt," he cried.

"Buy another," answered Devon as she sat down on the quilt.

"Need help with anything else?" JR answered no and that he could take care of it. After removing the rest of his things, he slowly sat on the quilt, took Devon in his arms, and began kissing her. He gently laid her back and began kissing her all over. He found her lips again and asked her if this was what she wanted. Devon said nothing as he unhooked her bra and removed it. He fondled her breasts as he gazed into her eyes for some sign that she liked what he was doing. When he saw nothing, he began to suck on her nipples. She could hear him moaning as he went from one breast to the other. Fearing he was getting too close to go on, he slid down to her stomach and started to slide her panties off. As he got them partway down, a silver packet slid out. He picked it up and asked her what it was.

"Don't you recognize a condom wrapper?" she said.

"You mean I have to use this?" he said, looking astonished.

"Only if you want to finish this," she said seriously.

"No woman has ever made me use a condom," he said angrily.

"Then this night is over," said Devon as she stood up, put her clothes on, and left, leaving JR sitting on the quilt filled with rage.

4

Sᴀʀᴀʜ ᴀɴᴅ Dᴇᴠᴏɴ ʜᴀᴛᴇᴅ the summer months. Devon was always busy at the lodge, and Sarah helped her mother canning vegetables that she grew in her small garden or the vegetables she received by exchanging them for her eggs. Either way, Sarah was not happy. She couldn't wait for school to begin when she and Devon could see each other every day. At the end of summer and just before winter, she and Devon had time to spend together. Sometimes Sarah was allowed to stay over at the lodge. It didn't happen often, but when it did, what fun the girls had, running up the mountain, visiting the horse farm, and visiting another of their friends that lived close by. The meals that were served at the lodge even when there were not many guests was like a feast to Sarah, always culminating in spectacular desserts. Sarah rarely got dessert at her house unless it was pie. That was all her father liked, so that was what she got. At the lodge, there were brownies, cheesecakes, coconut cakes, and more. *Yes,* she thought, *Devon had it made living here at the lodge.*

Summers passed quickly for the two girls, and now they were eleven. Nothing much changed for them except they heard that JR got married, he got another girl pregnant, and this time she wasn't going away. Sarah listened when her mother and father spoke about it when they thought she was upstairs and couldn't wait to tell Devon. The new bride thought she was going to live like a queen in the big house, but Russell Sr. had different ideas. He gave JR and his wife the small bungalow that was sometimes used by overnight guests his father invited up from the city. Sarah's father said JR's wife was a "real piece of work." Whatever that meant. She and Devon heard all about the fancy party they had at the big house. Course no one they knew was invited; but Mrs. Ogden, the florist in town who did most of the arrangements for the lodge, also did the floral arrangements for the wedding and let slip a few things when Devon was there to help her. Devon worked at the flower shop whenever she could; Mrs. Ogden was teaching her how to make the flower arrangements and some things about running a shop. Even at eleven, Devon knew that Mrs. Ogden wouldn't be running the shop for much longer. She was already in her sixties, and since she was the only florist in town—well, the only florist who did quality work anyway—Devon knew she would love to own the shop.

Mrs. Ogden had Devon filled small dishes with wet floral foam and filled them with greens, and then Mrs. Ogden would place all the flowers in them. She remarked that with all the money the Ledgers had, she would have thought they could have spent more on the flowers. Instead of roses or orchids, they were to be just some carnations and baby's breath. Devon thought they looked very nice, and they did, but not for a Ledger wedding. Even the bride's bouquet was to be of miniature carnations and baby's breath with some ivies. Still, Mrs. Ogden made sure they were just as beautiful as any other she made. She said that there was only a short honeymoon planned because JR had to make sure the stone fruit was harvested. The new Mrs. Ledger made her feelings known loud and clear to anyone who would listen that this was not the way she expected to be treated since she was now a part of the Ledger family; since everyone in town knew she had her sights set on JR for years and probably got pregnant just so she could force him to marry her. They just all walked away whenever they saw her coming. If she thought she was due the respect of a Ledger, she sure got it wrong.

Sometime in January, Devon and Sarah heard that JR had a daughter, but for the girls, it didn't mean a whole lot. They were too busy learning to ski and going sleigh riding and ice-skating. Neither Sarah nor Devon really liked the winters cold; the spring and fall were their favorite times of the year. The spring, with all the new shades of green and the trees flowering, there always seemed to be the sweet smell of perfume in the air; and of course there were the pollywogs, newly hatched in the stream, that the girls caught in glass jars to bring home and, like the years before, were told to bring them right back where they got them. They would check on them from time to time to see how close they were from turning into frogs. It was spring, and in a few months, school would be out. Even though fall meant going back to school, they loved the colors of the leaves and raked them into huge piles and jumped in them. Sarah's father used the leaves in the compost piles, so when they were done playing, they had to load them in a cart and dump them. Summers meant work again, but occasionally they found some free time and walked all the way up to the big house to see everyone get ready for the foxhunt. Sarah had gotten used to hearing the horn blow each time there was to be a hunt and seeing all the hounds barking and all the riders dressed in their fancy red coats; but to Devon, it was like watching a movie. Trying not to be noticed by Mr. Ledger or the riders, she would wait for them to ride out then try to ask anyone of the farm hands all she could about the sport. One of the oldest workers Mr. Ledger employed was a man named Carl Barnes; Carl worked for the Ledgers for over twenty years and was the only man Russell Sr. trusted to make sure the hunt went off well. As master of foxhounds, it was Russell Sr.'s responsibility to operate the sporting activity as well as maintain the kennels. Carl was the person who bred the hounds that were used for the hunt, a mix of American and English foxhounds. Carl gave his girls names like Patience and Venus, and the male dogs were called names like Valor, Hero, and Winston. Carl explained to Devon that the huntsman was responsible for directing the hounds during the course of the hunt with the help of the whipper. He kept the hounds together by the use of a long whip, but the real trick to keeping the hounds in line was the horn. The long rolling blow told the hounds to come back, and the short blow let the hounds and staff know that the master had changed directions. Two blows, one right after the other, summoned the staff if they were needed. Most of the people who came to ride owned their own horses. These tall field hunters had the ability to clear large obstacles, such as wide ditches or tall fences, and had the stamina to keep up with the hounds. Foxhunting was an old sport, both George Washington and Thomas Jefferson kept packs of hounds; today the sport was called fox chasing. The purpose was not to actually kill the fox but to enjoy the thrill of the chase. As a rule, foxes were not pursued once they have gone to ground, which meant simply that they had gotten into a den and were well hidden. Russell Sr. endeavored to maintain the fox population and habitats, as much as possible always providing new challenges for the riders.

Carl was just full of information that Devon took back to Sarah, but Sarah wasn't the least bit interested. The older the two became, the more Sarah was interested in her hair or her clothes, hoping the boys would take notice. Devon wasn't there yet; she was still interested in learning as much as she could about animals, the flower shop, and the workings of the lodge. Devon had plans, and right now, they didn't include boys.

5

DEVON WAS LIKE A sponge soaking up any and all information she could get to improve her knowledge of the three things that were important to her. While Carl continued to share his vast knowledge of animals large and small, Mrs. Ogden was pleased when Devon could put together a floral arrangement almost as well as her own, and working at the lodge rounded out her training. Devon knew what she wanted, and nothing changed that; not Sarah's whining when Devon refused to spend hours talking about hairstyles or the newest color of lipstick or walking around, hoping to catch the eye of some boys who were also walking around looking for the girls. Devon's plans were for success, not partying.

As the girls reached their senior year in high school, they remained friends but stopped spending as much time together. Sarah had a steady boyfriend and was having a difficult time keeping her grades up. Her parents feared she would not be accepted at a decent college, which was all right with Sarah. She didn't want to leave anyway, and besides, she had no clue what she wanted to do after high school. Her parents' greatest fear was that she would want to get married to the jerk she called her boyfriend who they knew was headed nowhere. They wanted more for their daughter but feared the worse. In the end, they all agreed that Sarah should go to vocational school to become a hairdresser. The course was only eight months, and Sarah was sure she could do that. She did, and after graduating, found a job in one of the local hair salons as Devon finished her first year in college. As Devon started her second year, Sarah had moved out of her parents' house; and she and the loser, as her father referred to him, got an apartment together with Sarah paying the bills because he kept getting fired from his latest job for always being late or high. No one could tell Sarah anything; she loved him and said he would be all right if everyone just gave him a chance. Everyone gave him a chance. That wasn't the problem. He just didn't give a damn as long as Sarah paid the bills and was ready to have sex whenever he wanted it. Life was all good for him. Even Devon couldn't make Sarah see how he was using her; but she wouldn't listen, so Devon stopped trying.

6

Devon was caught off guard when JR showed up at the flower shop a few days after their brief encounter at the local bar. He was so handsome and knew it, but he still took Devon's breath away. She thought of their last night together after leaving JR because he wouldn't wear the condom. She had dressed and got into her car and drove away. A half mile or so, she had to pull off the road because she started shaking. Devon started to cry. She couldn't believe that she had done something as careless as getting ready to have sex with a perfect stranger. Yes, she knew who JR was, but she didn't know the man. Who was this other person that took over her body and made her do something she herself would never do? What was she doing? Was it the fact that after all these years she still had that schoolgirl crush on him? She still had the handkerchief he gave her to put on the scratch she had gotten from his dog Beaver when she was eight. Why had she kept it all these years, washed and pressed with his initials RL prominently on one corner? She kept it in a little wooden keepsake box her mother bought her for Christmas the year before. She kept it there because the little box had a lock and key, and she knew it would be safe because she alone knew where the key was hidden. JR looked around the shop to see if there was anyone else there. Luckily for him, there was no one. Mrs. Ogden had gone off to the bank, and there were no customers in the store. After JR assured himself that they were alone, he approached her.

"You want to tell me what that was all about the other night? Are you freaking crazy or something? You sure got a lot of balls walking out on me," he said angrily.

"I wouldn't have if you just wore the condom," said Devon defiantly.

"You're just a goddamn tease, that's what you are. You pull that stunt on all the guys you go home with," he said, raising his voice.

"Raising your voice will get you nowhere," said Devon. "And no, I don't do that to all the boys I go home with. Just those that refuse to wear the condom."

"So what do we do about this?" said JR.

"What do we do about what?" Devon answered back.

"Don't be coy. You know damn well what I'm talking about," he said.

"Well, let's see. Dinner may be a good way to apologize for being an ass," she replied.

"I'm the one who should apologize. I think you got that a little backward here. I'm not taking you anywhere," he said as his face got redder and redder with anger.

"Do what you got to do, JR. It makes no difference to me," said Devon calmly; and with that, he stormed out of the shop. Devon smiled. She got him, and he knew it. A few days later, JR called the shop, asking for Devon. Mrs. Ogden called Devon to the phone and said the caller wouldn't tell her his name. Devon knew who it was. She answered the phone, trying to remain calm, but her heart was racing.

"Devon, this is JR. Where do you want to go for dinner?"

"Somewhere posh, I think. I haven't been dressed up in a while. I'll leave it up to you, JR. I'm sure you must have dined somewhere besides the local greasy spoon," said Devon casually.

"Fine. Saturday I'll pick you up at the lodge at seven," he said as he hung up the phone. There it was again, her heart beating louder than a drum. Why did he affect her so? She knew his reputation. Why did she even want to bother with him? Did she see something redeeming in him that no one else saw? Did that one event when she was eight cloud her judgment and let her believe there was another side to him? She knew this was dangerous. Devon rarely took chances. What was it about this man that made her want to walk that fine line between safety and danger? All she knew was that being near him made her blood run hot. Her body desired him, and she couldn't stop now if she wanted to. All she did know was that this had to play out, and Devon thought she knew the ending before it started.

JR arrived promptly at seven and entered the lodge and asked for Devon. She had been waiting nearby at one of the tables so she could see him arrive. She didn't want him to have to wait too long because of her parents. She knew as soon as they found out who she was dating, all hell would break loose. She quickly walked up to him and said they should go. JR made a joke that she must have been ashamed for people to see her with him.

When they got into the car, Devon told him it wasn't just anyone, it was her parents. He told her that they would find out sooner or later; this was a small town, and everyone knew who JR was seeing. Devon told him she much rather they found out later, and could he please change the subject. She wanted to enjoy the night, not spend it worrying about what her parents would say. JR laughed.

"So our little Devon is afraid of something after all," he said, almost gloating.

"Don't look so smug," she answered. "My parents mean the world to me, and I don't like deceiving them, but telling them right now would only result in an argument. One that I'd like to avoid for as long as possible."

"And we sure wouldn't want that, would we?" he replied.

"Don't be smart, JR. You know how bad your reputation is."

"Then why the hell are you going out with me? Do you want trouble with your parents? I don't think so. Then why, Devon? Why put yourself right in the middle of the beehive?" he asked.

"I don't know, JR," she yelled at him angrily. "Maybe I'm just tired of being the good girl, the responsible girl, the I-have-a-plan-and-am-sticking-to-it girl. I just want some fun for once, fun without looking at the future consequences all the time. Does that make any sense?"

"Yes, it does. I've lived my entire life that way. Most of the time, it was good. But on occasion, I made a real mess of things, things

I can't change. So think long and hard before you do something you'll regret."

"I think if I don't do it then I'll regret it," said Devon.

"Do what you got to do, Devon," he answered. Dinner that evening was a surprise for Devon. She thought there would be more awkward silence moments. She never expected that she and JR would have so much to talk about, but they talked and laughed the entire evening. Somewhere toward the middle of the evening, JR stopped trying so hard to be charming and just relaxed; something he rarely did with women. He created a reputation for himself, one that served him well, but this night was different. He felt different with Devon. He didn't feel as if he needed to prove anything to her. The experience was pleasurable, and JR wasn't the least upset when after dinner, Devon asked him to take her home. Usually after spending money, a lot of money on dinner, he expected to claim his reward; and that usually meant spending the rest of the night in bed, and he would decide when the evening was over. Devon said good night at the door to the lodge and told him she had a most enjoyable evening and perhaps they could do it again sometime. She kissed JR on the cheek, turned, and went inside, leaving him standing in the cold with a smile on his face. After he got into his car, he thought about what she just did and couldn't contain his laughter. He laughed so hard he had tears in his eyes. As he wiped his eyes, he said to himself that this was going to be one hell of a ride. The next day, he sent her two dozen yellow roses. When her father accepted them and called Devon, he asked her who they were from. After she read the card and laughed, she figured she might as well get it over with and told him they were from her date last night. Again, her father asked who sent them. Devon's relationship with her parents had always been close; mostly because she worked hard, stayed out of trouble, and did as she was told. But now that she was twenty-one, she began challenging them; not often, but on occasion. Devon knew instinctively that her parents would be unhappy when she told them that she was seeing JR, but she wanted to tell them herself. She didn't want them to hear it from anyone else.

"I had a date with JR Ledger last night, Dad. And before you give me the lecture on what a scoundrel he is, just let me say this.

I have always tried to do what you and Mother wanted even if I sometimes disagreed, but I think I have earned the right to decide for myself who I would like to go out with. Yes, I know all the gossip that surrounds JR. I've heard it since I was a child, but I'm not a child now, and I can decide for myself. Nothing has changed in my plans for the future—finish college, get my dog grooming school out of the way, and hopefully buy the flower shop from Mrs. Ogden. JR is just a bit of fun, nothing more. So please let's not argue about it. I know mother will hit the ceiling when she finds out, but I'm hoping you can relieve her fears before she makes a big thing out of it. Please, Dad, trust me. I know what I'm doing."

"Do you, Devon? Do you really?" said her father. "He's no good. Can't you see that? He has ruined more people's lives. I have to say I don't want you to see him again. Am I making myself clear?" It was unlike her father to get so emotional and forbid her to do anything; she couldn't remember the last time he did.

"I know what I'm doing, Dad," said Devon

"No, you don't!" yelled her dad.

"Dad, you're making a scene now. Keep your voice down," said Devon, but her father continued on until Devon promised she wouldn't see him again. She knew she would, but right now, she had to make her father stop his ravings.

7

Devon didn't hear from JR for two days. She had thought about calling him to thank him for the roses but changed her mind. She wanted to keep him off-balance and not act in the typical way other women would act, gushing over the phone about how beautiful the flowers were and how thoughtful of him to send them. Ugh. When the phone rang, she answered it but put him on hold after letting him wait five minutes. She was surprised by his demeanor. She expected to be chastised for letting him wait, but instead he was relaxed and unruffled. He asked politely how she was and if he caught her at a bad time. She told him that every time lately seemed to be a bad time; between the lodge and the flower shop, she felt like she was always running in six directions. He laughed and told her she needed some downtime and could she get free for dinner. She told him she could, but it would have to be an early evening because she had to be at the flower shop in the morning to get the rest of the flowers done for the Sullivan-Thorpe wedding on Saturday. He didn't complain, just asked what time he should pick her up. She told him she should be able to be ready by six thirty, and he said he'd be there. Devon was a little surprised by his behavior. Were her tactics working? Was she keeping him off-balance, or was he playing the same game with her?

Devon was waiting for JR outside so she wouldn't get into another argument with her mother. Her father must have told her that she was seeing JR. Her father told her to let Devon have some space, but her mother wouldn't let it go. She was like a bulldog with a bone, but this time Devon found the strength inside to ignore her mother's ravings about her dating JR. As soon as he pulled up, Devon jumped in and told him to go.

"Something got your pants on fire, missy?" he said to her.

"Don't be funny, JR. I just didn't want a scene with my mother," she snapped back.

"Got ya. Got a lecture about dating the worst scoundrel in the world, I bet."

"Something like that. Can we please change the subject. I've had enough questions for one day." JR smiled but didn't say any more. He drove south. Devon was going to ask him where they were going but decided to let it go and be surprised. They rode along in silence for ten minutes until JR felt that Devon finally felt relaxed. He asked about the flowers she was making for the wedding. Devon humored him and told him about all the corsages and the bride's bouquet, knowing full well he could care less, but she found it comforting that he asked. Then she remembered to thank him for the roses. Why yellow, she asked him. He answered that she just didn't seem like the red rose kind of girl.

"All the Ledgers have been invited to the wedding, even me. I guess when you put out as much money as her father has for this wedding, you make sure the people you invite are solvent enough to leave a hefty gift. I don't think it's something I want to do anyway. Not my kind of thing. But I hear old Mom and Dad are going. It's just their kind of thing. A chance to come down off the hill and touch elbows with the common folk," said JR with a laugh.

"So what's your kind of thing?" she asked.

"Just what I'm doing. Nice peaceful night, quiet ride, hopefully a pleasant dinner, and a beautiful woman to share it with. What more could you ask for?" he answered.

"Sounds lovely," said Devon, "but don't you miss a lot trying to avoid crowds?"

"Whatever it is, it can't be more important than this." He laughed. "You haven't asked where we're going," he said. "I guess your day was really that bad." Devon just sighed and laid her head back on the seat.

"Anything you want to talk about? You may not know it, but I'm a pretty good listener," he said.

"Are you, JR? Are you really? Because all I've ever heard about you has been that you were totally absorbed in yourself. Everything else took second seat. Why would you want to listen to me complain about my day?"

"If I told you I cared, would you believe me?" he said.

"Funny, but I think I would. I don't know why I would, but I would," answered Devon, looking at him smiling. "Don't look at me that way. We both know there's a Dr. Jekyll as well as a Mr. Hyde in there, and allowing your compassionate side to show occasionally is not that bad, you know."

"Oh, Devon, I've lived the last thirty-six years allowing Hyde to run loose. I'm not sure what is me or him anymore," said JR sadly.

"You know, JR. Down deep, you know," replied Devon.

"Devon, I think if I had met someone like you when I was younger, maybe I would have turned out differently." As they drove along, they passed a sign that read Woodstock. Devon wondered what they were doing in this small arts and crafts town but was completely surprised when they parked on a side street and walked around the corner to a small vegetarian bistro. They entered and were greeted by the hostess who sat them in the back corner table. She smiled at JR and handed them each a menu.

"You've been here before?" asked Devon.

"Yes, but never with a date," he answered.

"Just out trolling?" she asked.

"Now see. That remark is what I would expect from everyone else, not you," he said angrily. "It's a nice place, food's good, no one knows me, and I can sit and enjoy a meal."

"I'm sorry. You're right. I shouldn't have said that. Please just chalk it up to my bad day. I really am sorry," said Devon apologetically.

"Apology accepted," he said.

"So what do you recommend? I've never eaten in a vegetarian restaurant before, but everything looks so good," she said. Most things on the menu had hand drawn pictures of vegetables next to each item.

"No laughing, but I especially like the leek and onion quiche. And yes, before you say it, real men do eat quiche. They just never eat it around people they know," he said, grinning.

"Well, it sounds good to me. I'll have it to, and I promise not to tell anyone should they ask," said Devon, trying not to laugh.

"You realize you're letting me see that other side of you again, don't you?"

"Something tells me I'll be all right," he answered. The evening couldn't have been more enjoyable. The food was as good as JR claimed, and no one in the restaurant seemed to take notice of them in the corner. Devon soon found out that JR had a great sense of humor and was also surprised by his interest in other things. He liked to fish, both deep sea and quiet lake, and promised to take her sometime. He said a nice afternoon was slowly drifting around the lake, watching the red bobber play in the water as some fish attempted to take the worm, then a small picnic on the shore. A great way to spend the day was lying back, watching the clouds float by, and pretending that this was all there was; no other people, no work, no deadlines, and no noise. JR said he could never have enough silence, which surprised Devon. JR always seemed to be in the middle of one controversy or another; maybe that was why he liked the sound of silence. This was a complicated man; a man of many facets. And as they sat quietly and sipped their coffee, Devon herself realized that the sound of silence was something she missed too.

The ride home took longer because JR took all the back roads he could. Devon expected him to drive straight back to his bungalow and get what he didn't get on their first night, but they meandered along following some roads that Devon never knew existed. They talked about many things but nothing to do with work either his or hers. They talked about books, about places in the world they would like to see, even about politics. Surprisingly enough they found that they both enjoyed many of the same things. JR confided in her that he wished he had a do-over for all the stupid things he did in his life and how he got lost somewhere along the way. Devon told him that it was never too late for a do-over, but JR said he was too tired and didn't have the fight anymore. Devon felt tears well up in her eyes; here was a man who supposedly had it all, and all he felt was nothingness, emptiness, and darkness. How sad he was. They rode in silence until he pulled up in front of the lodge.

"Here you are back safe and sound," he said. "I'm sure Mom has been pacing the floor. Probably thought I took you out and chopped you to bits or something."

"That's not funny, JR."

"I know and I'm sorry. This night has meant more to me than you can imagine, Devon. Now go on get some sleep. You said you had an early morning."

"Yes, I did. This night has meant a lot to me also. Thank you for letting Dr. Jekyll and I have a wonderful evening. I hope I can see him again," said Devon as she kissed him on the lips and got out of the car. She barely had time to close the door as he sped away. Had he let her see too much? Sadness overcame Devon as she stood watching the red taillights get smaller and smaller as he drove away. Tears rolled down her cheeks, and she quickly wiped them away before entering the lodge. Seeing tears on their daughter's face would be just what her parents would expect, and they would never understand that nothing happened while she was out with JR. They would automatically jump to the worst conclusions, and nothing Devon could say would avert another confrontation with them. She made sure her eyes were dry and her face cleared of any tears, then opened the door. As she suspected, her mother was waiting at the counter. Not wanting another battle, she just smiled and said good night and that she had to leave early in the morning to finish the flowers for the wedding. Her mother didn't smile back or say good night. She just stood there looking slightly perplexed. It was only ten o'clock, and she was home already. Could she have been wrong? Maybe they weren't seeing each other romantically, but she knew that this was not going to end well for her daughter.

8

Devon worked feverously on the wedding flowers. Mrs. Ogden said they couldn't have been more beautiful than if she made them all herself. She was so proud of Devon. Devon knew Mrs. Ogden was giving her more responsibility in the daily running of the shop. Devon had to finish this last semester then go to New York for six months to take a course in the dog grooming business, and then they could have the discussion about Devon buying the business from her. Mrs. Ogden's health was not getting any better; she was tired all the time and hoped she could hang on until Devon finished school. She envied Devon. Here she was at the start of her career, and Mrs. Ogden was at the end of hers. Devon had always known exactly what she wanted to do with her life, the flower shop, the pet store, and the grooming business and still help her parents with the lodge; and if she could find the money someday, a no-kill animal sanctuary. Her two years in college gave her all the training she needed for business management and the extra year for accounting. Mrs. Ogden envied her single-minded drive but sometimes wondered if it didn't come with a heavy price. She had little time to socialize with her friends and was losing precious time to enjoy just being a young lady. Taking on so much at her age, Mrs. Ogden couldn't help but think that one day, Devon would look back and say to herself, "Did I give up too much, and did I have fun?"

Devon boxed the wedding flowers and gave them to their delivery man. Mrs. Ogden said that there were no more orders for the day and was closing the store at noon and would reopen on Monday. She congratulated Devon for doing such a fine job on her first wedding flowers and told her to go have some fun and that she deserved it. Devon wasn't quite sure what to do. There was always something she could be doing at the lodge to help her parents but decided instead to take Mrs. Ogden's advice and have some fun. She dialed JR's number and asked him if he was busy. He told her he was and that he was overseeing his hands bringing in the cherry crop; another few days and they would be overripe. Too bad, she told him. Mrs. Ogden closed the shop for the day, and she needed some fun. JR said he would like to oblige, but the cherries didn't pick themselves, and he had to be there, but maybe he would be free after eight when it got too dark for the men to pick any more. If they did go out, he would have to call it an early night because he had to be up at dawn to get the rest of the crop in. Devon was disappointed but told him she understood and for him to go to bed early and that she would connect with him another time.

Guess I'll head for the lodge, she told herself. Devon arrived at the lodge and caught her parents just sitting down for lunch.

"Hi, guys, anything good?" she asked.

"Darling, how nice to see you," said her mother. "Are you done at the flower shop?"

"Yes, Mrs. Ogden closed at noon. She said we did enough for one day, so I thought I'd see what you were up to and hopefully have a decent lunch."

"Dad and I decided to splurge and have the grilled salmon with a salad. Would you like some? I'll tell the cook," said her mother.

"That's okay, Mom. I'll get it myself, and I'll join you." Before she began college, it was one of her dad's rules that they eat at least one meal together each day to stay connected, he said. Devon got her meal from the cook and sat down with her parents.

"Well, this is great," said her dad. "My two favorite ladies sharing a meal with me. I can't remember the last time we all sat and ate a meal together as a family. This is really nice."

"Yeah, Dad, this is nice," said Devon. "I remember when we always had at least one meal together, you're right. I miss it."

"So what are you going to do with your free afternoon?" asked her mother.

"I don't know. I could always study. Final exams will be here before long, not that I'm worried about any of them. For some reason, this last semester has been the easiest one I've had so far. I think I'm going to do really well in my finals, then three weeks of freedom, and off to New York and grooming school."

"You're still set on doing that?" asked her father.

"Yep, nothing's changed, Dad. The flower shop, the pet store, and the grooming salon. I know it's a lot, but that's what I've been working so hard for, and one day I'll have it, along with the no-kill animal shelter," said Devon.

"Funny, I don't remember being that ambitious when I was your age," said her father. "It must come from your mother's side."

"Well, wherever it comes from, that's the plan," replied Devon as she polished off her lunch.

"Honey, it's a little slow around here. Nothing your father can't handle, so how about you and I go spend some quality mother-and-daughter time."

"What did you have in mind?" asked Devon.

"Maybe a little shopping. We could go to the Galleria in Poughkeepsie and get you some new clothes for New York. Can't have you looking like a hillbilly now, can we?"

"I would love spending the afternoon with you, Mom, but clothes aren't necessary. You and dad are already paying for school."

"And you will be supporting yourself with the money you've saved from all the work you have been doing here and in the flower shop, so I think there's still a little money left in the budget, right, honey?"

"If I said no, would it matter?" said her dad. "Go on, you two. Have a fun afternoon, but watch the budget." Devon got up and gave her father a kiss and a hug.

"I love you, Dad," she said.

"Back at ya, kiddo," he said. Warren watched as his wife and daughter left the lodge. Suddenly, he felt quite old. His baby was ready to leave the nest and take on the world. He envied her drive to achieve the goals she set for herself, but he missed the little girl that used to climb up in his lap and fall asleep while he read her a story. It seemed ages ago now as he watched the tall, beautiful, self-confident woman she had become. He was so proud of her and realized that he hadn't told her that in some time. The next time he saw her, he would be sure she knew just how much he loved her and how proud he was of her. Devon was one in a million. No parent could ask for a better child, and he would do whatever it took to help her make her dream come true.

9

DEVON AND HER MOM had a great day together. Her mother insisted to buy way too many clothes for her, but Devon could see how much she was enjoying spoiling her only child. Devon always wished she had a brother or sister, but despite many tries and many miscarriages, Devon was destined to be an only child. She worried about her parents. She had never been away from them before, and going to school in New York City was going to be harder on them than her, but she promised them that she would try to come home every other weekend. She had to come home; she knew JR wanted her to. He already said he wouldn't come to the city to see her, so she had to come home. After an entire afternoon of trying on clothes, Devon said she quit. What they needed now was to go back and find that ice cream shop and get the largest banana split they could get, and for once, her mom agreed. Usually her mother would pass on dessert, always watching her figure, which was a puzzle to Devon; her mom was a beautiful 5'6", 130-pound dynamo. Devon always thought her mother was beautiful, but now as she was older, she really appreciated her even more. She always wished she had her mother's blond hair instead of the copper curls she had to fight with every morning. Her father said she got her red hair from his side. Most of the relatives from her father's side were of Irish descent, while her mother's people were Scandinavian. Since there was nothing she could do anything about her hair color or the few freckles across her cheeks, she stopped thinking about it.

It was just in times like this did she see her mother in a new light. She so wanted to make her proud. She didn't know why it was so important, but it was.

Devon and her mom returned to the lodge just after dinner. Neither of them were hungry because they both polished off a banana split just an hour before. Devon kissed her dad as she ran through the lodge and up to her room to put the many bags she had away. She ran back downstairs and saw her mom and dad deep in conversation.

"Is Mom telling you how we broke the bank?" Devon laughed.

"She did mention that she went a little overboard," said her father, "but we were just talking about the phone message I took for you. It was from JR saying he'd pick you up at eight thirty. I didn't know you had a date with him again?"

"I didn't. He said he had cherries to bring in, and I told him I'd catch up with him another time," she answered.

"Well, he seems to have gotten the cherries in after all," replied her father.

"I guess so. I'll go up and change."

"Darling," said her mother, "your father and I really think this is unwise your dating JR. You know his reputation, and I'm just not comfortable with you seeing him."

"I know, Mom, but we had this conversation before, and I promise I'll be fine. Don't worry," said Devon as she ran up the stairs to change. JR was on time as usual. You would think with his reputation that he would be perpetually late, but he never was. Devon ran out to the car instead of making him park and come inside. She was just trying to avoid a scene with her parents, but she knew that at some point in time he would have to come in and talk to them, but not tonight. It was already late, and she wanted to spend as much time with him as she could.

"Hi," she said as she jumped into the car. "I thought I told you to go to bed and have an early night."

"You did and I thought about it but decided I'd rather spend an hour or two with you rather than go to bed," he answered.

"I hope we're not doing anything fancy. I didn't know what to wear."

"You're fine," he replied. "So how did your day go with your mother? Your father told me the two of you went shopping for clothes."

"Mom didn't want to send me to New York looking like a country bumpkin. At least that's what she said. I think she just wanted to spend some time together because she knows I'll be leaving in three weeks. Finals this week, then three weeks of freedom except for the flower shop, then off to the city for the final phase of my education."

"I don't think I ever met anyone as driven as you are, Devon," said JR.

"Yeah, that's what my dad said too. I just know what I want, and I know I have to work for it."

"I hope I fit in there someplace," said JR.

"Oh, you do." Devon giggled. "So where are we off to? Mom and I just had banana splits a few hours ago, so I'm really not that hungry."

"Me neither. I had a sandwich earlier. I thought we would just go down to the river café and get a drink if that's all right."

"Fine with me," replied Devon. The little café and bar was on the Hudson River with an outside deck area and an inside area, plus it connected to a small marina where people pulled up in their boats for dinner and drinks. Devon followed JR to an outside table by the water. A series of wooden cross pieces were strung with those tiny white lights they use on Christmas trees, and large planters were filled with an assortment of colored flowers and greens. Devon noticed the flowers wherever she went, getting ideas for future reference. The waitress took their drink order and placed a bowl of peanuts on the table. Shells littered the floor all over the deck; she wouldn't want to be the person that swept them up at night. Her father had tried that once in their bar at the lodge, but it proved to be more trouble than it was worth. Devon was glad when he decided it was too much work cleaning up at night.

"It's so beautiful here. I couldn't wait until I turned twenty-one so I could come down here. It's just not the same coming here and having a Coke. Some of my friends from school would make me come with them so I could be the designated driver."

"Well, you may not have liked it, but it was a smart move. I've seen too many people think they can sit and drink all night then get in their car and head for home. Lots didn't make it in one piece either," said JR.

"You never got too drunk to drive?"

"Nope. Always know your limitations. Live longer that way," he said. Then he got really quiet as the waitress brought their drinks. Devon waited. JR just stared out into the water as if in deep thought, then turned back to look at her.

She's so beautiful, he thought to himself. *What have I gotten into, and how will I stand it when she leaves? God, I want to take her in my arms and kiss her. Just kiss her. That's enough for now. Sex can wait.* He couldn't believe he just thought that. There was a time when that was all he wanted from a woman, but Devon was different. She had gotten under his skin and made him feel different; not the same man as he was with other people. He thought more about it. He hadn't even seen another woman since his first meeting with her. He smiled.

"You look like the cat that swallowed the canary, JR. What are you thinking about?" asked Devon.

"Oh, just how beautiful you are and how I'll miss you when you're gone," he answered.

"Right," she answered. "You'll probably find another woman the first day I'm gone."

"Don't know if I will," he answered seriously, then gazed back at the water. They both were silent for some time, each looking for the right words, but none came. When Devon had finished her drink, JR said he'd like to go. He stopped at the lodge, putting his car in park, then reach over to kiss her. Devon met him halfway and felt the taste of scotch in his mouth. As she pulled away, she paused, then asked if they were all right.

"We're fine, Dev. Just chalk up the night to this old man's fatigue, okay."

"All right, if you're sure that's all it is," she asked.

"I'm sure," he said. "Good night." Devon leaned forward and kissed him again then said good night and got out of the car, closing the door gently. She felt worried. Was he tired of her already? Had she done something or not done something? Her mind raced with all the things that could be wrong.

No, she said to herself, if it's over, it's over. Devon had a difficult time falling asleep and had bad dreams when she finally did.

10

On Sunday, Devon had a late breakfast and decided to study for her finals. Two on Monday, one on Tuesday, and two more on Thursday, and she was done. She had to work in the flower shop a half day on Tuesday and all day on Wednesday and Friday, but she was off Saturday. With a weekend free, her mind began to race. Could she convince JR to spend the weekend with her someplace, or would he have to work bringing in the stone fruit, this time it was peaches? She would call him on Tuesday after her exam and suggest they spend the weekend together; hopefully he would be in a better mood than the night before.

On Sunday afternoon, JR called and asked if she was busy and could get away for a few hours. She told him that she had been studying and would love a break. He told her he would pick her up around six. As usual, he was right on time; only this time he had parked the car and came into the lodge to get her. The first thing he saw when he entered the lodge was Devon's parents. There was no way he could avoid them and so headed straight for them.

"Evening, Mr. Taylor, Mrs. Taylor! Business seems to be doing well. Looks like you've got a full house," he said.

Devon's father was the first to speak. "Evening, JR! Yes, we do have a full house. Actually we are pretty well booked through September. The season started off slow but picked up nicely." As Devon's father spoke to JR, her mother turned and walked away.

She had no intention of making it seem like she approved of his seeing her daughter.

"I guess your wife isn't too pleased to see me," he said.

"I'm sorry, JR, but if truth be told, neither of us are too happy about it. We think you're too old for Devon, and your past, well, let's just say you've had a colorful one, and Devon's just starting out, if you know what I mean."

"I understand, Mr. Taylor. If I was in your shoes, I'd probably feel the same way. But know this, I've changed a lot since I've been seeing Devon. She makes me think before I act or say something stupid. I'm not sure what it is, but I know you don't have to worry about her. I promise I'll never hurt her."

"Well, I guess that's something. I hope you keep your word, JR. I really do," answered Devon's father. Just at that moment, Devon appeared. She looked a bit startled as she watched her father and JR talking.

Well, this can't be good, she said to herself as she approached them, trying to maintain an air of confidence.

"Father, JR," she said, "would I be correct in assuming that the two of you were talking about me? I thought I felt my ears ringing."

"No," said her father, "we were talking about the lodge and how we have it booked through September."

"Oh, my mistake then. See you later, Dad," she said as she walked away with JR following close behind.

"All right, what were you two really talking about?" she said to JR.

"The usual, you," he said.

"I just knew it," said Devon angrily. "They just won't stay out of my business."

"You have to look at it from their side, Devon. You're their fair-haired girl. The one all their hopes and dreams are pinned on. Of course they are going to scrutinize any man who comes into your life. Actually your father wasn't that bad, but your mom just walked away when she saw me," replied JR.

"Yeah, she has definitely made her feelings known," answered Devon. "Let's just forget them. My head is aching enough from all the studying I've been doing. I really don't need anything else on my mind."

"You ready for your finals?" he asked.

"I think so. I think I'll do pretty well in most of them. Accounting 2 may be a little tricky, but I know enough to run a business and keep a set of books, so even if I somehow manage to screw it up, I should still be all right," answered Devon. "Okay, enough of parents and school. What's up, JR?"

"Nothing much. I just had something I wanted to show you, that's all," he said.

"What is it?"

"No, it doesn't work like that. You'll just have to wait to see it."

"Can you at least tell me where we're going then?" she asked.

"Nope." They rode along for a while then Devon recognized the roads they were taking and surmised that they were going to his bungalow. She didn't say anything as they pulled into the driveway. She got out and followed him as he opened the door. Devon stepped inside and was so surprised.

"JR, it's beautiful. When did you do all this?" she asked.

"They have been working on it the last few weeks and just got it done on Saturday. You're the first one to see it completed," he said.

"Oh, it really is quite wonderful. What a difference." Devon was talking about the complete overhaul done to the house. "The whole thing looks so different. I just love the colors and the furniture style. I have to tell you that the colonial blue walls and early American furniture were really gross, but this is fantastic. Did you choose the colors and furniture?" she asked him.

"Sort of. I went to that paint and decorating shop in town, told them what I wanted the place to look like, and suggested the colors, and they filled in the rest. I thought it came out rather well. I never liked the way it was done before either but never had any incentive to change it until now. I especially want you to see the bedroom." Devon followed JR into the bedroom and saw that it was done in much the same manner as the living room, with soft sage on the walls and sleek, modern furniture that reflected a modern oriental feel.

"I'm guessing the bedroom was like the old living room?" she asked.

"Yep, colonial blue and early American. After seeing this, I don't know how I stood the other so long."

"What made you go for such a big change?" asked Devon.

"Oh, partly because I was just sick of it. It was depressing thinking about my married days living here and partly because of you."

"What did I have to do with it?" asked Devon.

"Don't you remember the first night we were here and you asked me if I took all my women into this bedroom and I said I had? I knew I didn't want our first time together to be in that old room. Then once I started thinking about it, I knew all of it had to be changed. I even had a new bed put in here. The kitchen has been stripped and new everything put in there also, even the bathrooms are done. I did this for you, Devon. Just for you."

"I'm speechless, JR."

"That will be a first. So you like it then?" he asked.

"What's not to like? It has such a wonderful, relaxing feel. Yes, JR, I love it, and I love that you did this all for me." With JR standing so close behind her, she guessed this was going to be the night they would finally make love.

"We just have to get something straight, JR. I will still ask you to use a condom."

"Hell's bells, girl, don't I deserve a little slack? You get my blood boiling, and then you go and get all cold on me. What gives?" he yelled.

"Look, JR, you've been with lots of partners, but you can't know who they might have been with, and I don't plan on getting any STDs," she said calmly.

JR yelled, "STDs!"

"Yes, sexually trans—"

"I know what the hell they are, and how the hell do I know I won't get anything from you?" he snapped back.

"Because I'm a virgin."

"Because you're a what?" he said.

"A virgin, dummy. I've never been with anyone before," answered Devon.

"Well, ain't this one for the books?" he said as he sat down on the bed. "Twenty-one and still a virgin. Who would have guessed it? What are you saving it for?" he said angrily.

"Why are you so angry? I thought it was a big thing for a guy to deflower a virgin."

"It may be to some, but I never found it especially enjoyable," he said.

"I'm sorry. I just wanted my first time to be with someone I cared about. I guess you could call me a little old-fashioned that way. I wanted to make love, not just have sex," said Devon.

"You take the cake, Devon. You really take the cake," he said as he stood up and took her hand. He walked her through the kitchen and told her to grab her bag. She asked where they were going, but JR never said another word until he dropped her off at the lodge and said good night. Devon watched as he pulled away. She knew she couldn't go inside with the tears rolling down her cheeks, so she took a short walk where she was sure no one would see her and cried. Once she felt better, she walked over to the pool to sit in one of the lounge chairs and tried to think about what just happened. It didn't make sense to her. JR's reputation with women and he didn't want her because she said she was a virgin. Devon pulled her knees up to her chest and cried some more and told herself that this must be the end.

11

Devon was extremely good at compartmentalizing; she would put the things she had to do in a box of their own and allow her full attention to be on the task at hand. She finished all her exams and was sure she did well on everything. She worked in the flower shop on Friday and was told by Mrs. Ogden that she was closing the shop from that Saturday until the following Monday for a short vacation. She wanted to go to see her sister in Pennsylvania before winter was upon them again. Devon was thrilled; that gave her plenty of time to get her things ready for her trip to New York and the grooming school. Mrs. Ogden asked her to pick up the flowers on Monday because she might be too tired from her trip back from Pennsylvania. Devon was so excited about going for the flowers, she had forgotten about JR for a while. As they closed the shop on Friday evening and put the vacation sign up, Devon started to unravel. She kissed Mrs. Ogden goodbye and walked to her car.

Now what, she thought to herself, *an entire week with nothing to do*? She knew she could find plenty of work around the lodge, but she really wanted some downtime before New York. She drove to the lodge and told her parents about Mrs. Ogden closing the shop for the week and that she may drive to New Paltz for a few days to see her girlfriend Rory, the one she would be staying with while attending school. Before Rory's parents bought their summer home, they had stayed at the lodge for a few summers, and that was how she and Devon became friends.

Rory was in her second year at Fordham University studying law and hoped to pass the bar and go into the family law firm. Both of her parents were lawyers. They had a beautiful home in the city, and when Devon told Rory she was taking the dog grooming class for six months, she asked her parents if Devon could stay with them. They were thrilled to have Devon stay with them, especially Mr. Stewart. Devon was the only one who would play chess with him. Both Mrs. Stewart and Rory found the game boring, but Devon found it challenging. Her father always kidded but used to say, "Put a challenge in front of Devon, and she was a happy camper." Her mom and dad had no problem about her going to visit Rory and frankly welcomed it; it would mean she would be away from JR. Devon called Rory and made plans to meet her on Saturday afternoon.

Devon stayed with Rory until Wednesday and confided in her about JR. Rory sided with her parents and told Devon to walk away now before it got serious and she got hurt. But Devon knew it was serious, and she was already hurt. With all their travel plans finalized, in two weeks, Devon's father would drive her to New Paltz on Saturday, and she would leave with the Stewarts on Sunday to drive back to the city. Devon had nothing else to do. She took her time driving back to the lodge. Her mother called and asked where she was and that JR had been by and was there anything she wanted her to tell him if he stopped by again? She said he seemed rather disturbed not finding her at home. Devon told her just to tell him if he showed up again that they didn't know when she would be home. Devon didn't let the phone call from her mother disturb her. She drove slowly and stopped at a few fruit and vegetable stands on the way home and bought a few things she thought would be good for dinner. She and her dad tried to plant a garden several times each spring, but the only ones who benefited were the animals. They came out at night and ate everything, so no more garden. Devon arrived home by five and had a nice dinner with her parents then went to her room. Her mother called her at seven and told her JR was back and did she want them to tell him she wasn't home yet, but Devon said no and that she would deal with him. She came down the stairs and watched as he paced back and forth. She wanted to feel sorry for him, but he hurt her, so she was reserving any emotion until she found out what he wanted.

"Evening, JR. Can I help you with anything?" she said, rather flippant.

"Yeah, we need to talk," he said, annoyed.

"So talk," she answered.

"Do you think we could go someplace a little more private?" he asked.

"Sure," was all she said and headed for the door, leaving JR still standing in the foyer.

"Get in the car," he snapped.

"I don't think so," said Devon. "I don't think I like your tone."

"Look," he said, "I'm sorry. Please get in the car." Devon got in the car as asked but said nothing. JR pulled away and drove them to his house. He opened the car door for her, which was a first, then ushered her into the house. She wasn't expecting what came next. JR pulled her into his arms and began kissing her; she couldn't stop herself and kissed him back. He began walking her toward the bedroom. Devon stopped just short of the bed. JR handed her a piece of paper, and as she began to read it, he began unbuttoning her blouse.

"Wait a minute. What's all this?" she asked.

"It's a report from my doctor. I had some blood work done, and the results say that I don't have any STDs or HIVs or anything transmittable. It's what you wanted, isn't it? So there you are, in black and white. As for the other thing, I guess I acted like an ass. I'm sorry if I was insensitive. I should have felt flattered, I suppose. It's just that I haven't dated anyone like you before. Most of the women I've dated had been there and done that. I didn't realize that there were still virgins in the world. I'm sorry." He looked so genuinely ashamed. Devon didn't know whether to laugh or cry.

"All right, let's forget everything and start again," said Devon as she began to unbutton his shirt.

"Could you leave the buttons on this one? This is another favorite." He laughed.

"I don't think I should tell you this, but I love you, Devon Taylor. You make my world seem right." Devon held her breath. She never expected him to say he loved her. She thought she was just another plaything for him, but she knew how to answer.

"Tell me again, JR," she said. He told her again as he held her close.

"And maybe I shouldn't tell you, but I love you, JR." They held each other closely. Then the phone rang.

"Don't answer it, JR," said Devon.

"I have to. Some damn workers probably screwed something up," he replied. JR answered the phone and was surprised to hear Devon's father on the other end. He told JR that Devon was needed at home immediately. JR relayed the message to Devon.

"I have to go home, JR. I don't want to, but I have to," she whispered.

"I know," was all he said.

"I hate this," she said. "Twenty-one and still afraid of my parents."

"You're not afraid of them. You're afraid of disappointing them. There's a difference," he said.

"But I want to stay here with you, to wake up in your arms, to feel your body next to mine when the sun comes up."

"Look, the situation's not the best, so we make the best of what we have," he answered.

"I can't believe you're so cavalier about it. Don't you want me to be with you all night?"

"Of course, I do, but we have to be realistic. I can't get away right now, and when I can, you'll be in New York. A few months from now, I'll be free, then we can plan a weekend together."

"Promise," she said

"I promise. Just let me tell you this. If I thought you could give up your parents, I'd say the hell with them and I'd pay for your school and whatever else you might need, but that wouldn't work, and you know it. Your parents are everything to you, and I think that's wonderful. I'd never do anything to spoil that. Sometimes I wished I had that kind of relationship with mine. Maybe then I wouldn't be so screwed up. What you have is beautiful. You need them, and they need you. That's just the way it is, so no rocking the boat. You got to do what you got to do, and for me, any minute we can find to spend together is all I can ask for."

"Who said you're all screwed up, JR? You make more sense than most people I know, and you're right about my parents. I love them, and I love you, and there's no way I could choose," replied Devon.

"And you'll never have to. I promise," he answered. "Now let's get you home."

12

DEVON OPENED THE DOOR to the lodge and found her mother and father waiting for her. *What gives,* she thought to herself, *everyone looks fine. What was the big emergency?*

"Hey, what's up?" said Devon. "What's so important you needed me to come home?"

Her father asked her to come into the office with him and her mother. They had something they needed to discuss with her, and it couldn't wait. Devon led the way to the office with her father and mother behind. Devon's father was the last to enter the room and quietly closed and locked the doors so no one could barge in on them.

"Wow, I must have really done it this time," said Devon jokingly.

"I'm sorry, darling," said her mother, seriously, "but we knew you and JR were getting too close, and we need to tell you something that is going to hurt you, but we need for you to know." Her mother began to cry, and her father put his arms around her for support. Her mother asked her to sit down, and she sat down next to her. Her mother pulled a tissue from a pocket and tried to dry her eyes.

"This is so hard for me, Devon. I somehow hoped you would never have to know this, but I guess I was wrong. Please bear with me, honey, while I tell you."

"Of course, Mom," said Devon, "you know you can tell me anything. I always loved the fact that we could talk to each other."

"Devon, the reason we don't want you to continue to see JR is—"
Her mother broke down and began to cry again. Her father came
over and put his arms around her.

"Devon, what your mother is trying to say is that JR is your
half brother. Your mother was raped when she was seventeen by
JR's father."

"What? Are you two crazy? How can you be so mean?" said
Devon, getting up. "I don't believe this."

"I know this is a lot for you to understand," said her father,
"but it's true, every word. We wouldn't lie to you about something
like this."

"Mom, Mom, is this true? Tell me. Is this true?"

"Yes, darling, it's true. When I was seventeen and about to
graduate high school, I was president of the Honor Society, and as
such, I was supposed to pick up a check of ten thousand dollars that
had been donated to the library by Mr. Ledger for new books. I
went to his house alone at around seven that evening. He answered
the door and asked me to come into the library for the check.
The house was so big, and he said that there wasn't anyone home,
that his wife was away for a few days, and the servants had the
night off. I remember thinking about how nice it must be to even
have servants, that they must live really well here. He offered me
something to drink, but I refused. He told me how beautiful I was
then sat down to write the check. When he got up, he placed the
check on the desk, and he, he grabbed hold of my arms and tried
to kiss me. I tried to pull away, but he was so strong and such a
big man. I couldn't. He pulled me to the floor, and he—" Devon's
mother began to cry again.

"He raped her, Devon. JR's father raped your mother. After he
was done, he handed her the check and told her to say nothing
to anyone because no one would believe her and it would cause
embarrassment for her family. So she said nothing. Then she
found out she was pregnant. She left one day and drove to her
grandmother's. She had always been close to her and the only one
she felt she could tell, and since her grandmother lived in Syracuse,
there would be no gossip here. They told her parents that she had
decided to go to school in Syracuse and live with her grandmother,

which was all right with them. I was already in school there, and that's where I met your mother. My father who owned the lodge at the time was great friends with her grandmother, and she confided in him the entire story. My father asked me to seek your mother out and keep my eye on her as she didn't know anyone in school or in town except her grandmother."

"Your father introduced himself to me at my grandmother's and told us what his father asked him to do. I was mortified with embarrassment, but your father was so kind and made me see that it wasn't my fault. We saw each other almost every day, and grandmother made sure he came for dinner a few times a week. Even though I was getting bigger, your father never made me feel ashamed about what happened to me, and we soon fell in love. We were married when I was seven months pregnant, and we lived with my grandmother until he finished school. I never wanted to return here, but your father was needed to help with the lodge, which was seeing more business. No one questioned who the father of my baby was because we had been married and away for almost four years. Even my parents thought your father was yours. It was so hard for me to go into town. I knew no one knew, but I was so frightened that I might run into the Ledgers, any of them. Your dad and I felt that you and JR might be getting to romantically involved, and we had to tell you before, well, before it went any further. I'm so sorry, my darling. I never wanted you to find out about this." Her mother once again leaned against her father and sobbed.

"This has been so difficult for your mother to watch you take off with JR and think about what you might be doing," said her father. Devon began to laugh.

"If you only knew how close we were. If you hadn't called when you did, we would have already been in bed," said Devon as she walked around the room laughing then crying. "Five minutes and I would have been having sex with my half brother." And with that said, she ran for the bathroom and threw up. When she returned after washing her face and mouth with water, she had stopped crying and went to her mother, sat down beside her and pulled her into her arms. With both of them wrapped around each other, they cried again. Devon cried for the pain her mother went through, and her mother because she knew she just broke her daughter's heart. Devon left her father and mother in the office. She left a brief note on the desk and ran to her car. Devon didn't know where she was running to but just knew she had to get away. She drove for hours until she was near Syracuse. She knew her parents would be franticly worrying about her, so she left a message that she was fine, and she just needed some alone time. She found a motel, checked in, and cried through the night. By morning, exhausted as she was, she knew what she had to do. It would be the hardest thing she ever did, but it had to be done. She drove back to the lodge, kissed her mother and father, and told them she was okay and needed some sleep, then she would go and talk to JR. Devon slept most of the day, got up, and showered and dressed. She felt weak and realized she hadn't had anything to eat since yesterday. She went into the kitchen and had some soup and half a sandwich; all of which she thought she would bring back up. The thought of almost having sex with her half brother was nauseating. She managed to keep the food down then told her parents she was going to see JR. Her father suggested she tell him to come to the lodge and they would tell him together, but she said it was something she needed to do herself. She drove to his bungalow, trying to find the words she would say when she saw him, but nothing came.

She got out of the car and rang the bell, and JR soon answered the door.

"I've been meaning to give you a key to the place, but I keep forgetting," he said. "Come on in. I also expected you back last night. What was so important at the lodge?"

"JR, we need to talk," whispered Devon.

"Sure, what do you want to talk about? How about waiting until we finished what we started last night?" he replied.

"No, JR, we won't be finishing what we started last night. In fact, after I explain something to you, we won't be seeing each other anymore."

"Explain what, Devon? And what the hell are you talking about?" he asked.

"When I got back to the lodge last night, my mom and dad asked to speak to me in private. My mother told me something that happened to her when she was seventeen. At least she tried to tell me. She was nearly hysterical, and my dad had to finish. She was broken, JR. All these years carrying it around, and it was because you and I were getting so close that she had to tell me. And I believe her, JR. I believe it all."

"What, what did she tell you, Devon? For Chrissake, tell me!" he yelled.

Devon started to cry, tears rolling down her cheeks. JR went to hold her, but she backed away from him.

"All right, Devon, what's going on?" he asked.

"My mother said that when she was seventeen, she was raped by your father, so that makes you and me, half brother and sister," she answered.

"What kind of crazy story is that? My father?"

"Yes, JR, your father! Mother had to go to the house to pick up a check he was giving to the school, and while she was there, he tried to kiss her. She tried to leave, but he pinned her down and raped her. The only one she ever told was her grandmother, and when she found out she was pregnant, she went to live with her in Syracuse and stayed with her. She and my father were married before I was born. It was over four years before they came back so Dad could work at the lodge, so no one questioned the fact that they had a daughter. No one knew, just my dad, and he raised me as his own and loved me. So you see why we will never be together, not ever, JR." JR was on his feet, pacing back and forth, nearly foaming at the mouth.

"If this is true, I'll kill him. I swear," said JR. "He has always tried to ruin my life, and now it looks like he really did it this time."

"I'm sorry, JR, but it's true. Goodbye, JR." Devon ran out the door. JR ran after her, but she was already in her car. He walked back in to his house, went into the living room, poured himself a very large glass of scotch, and plopped down in a chair. His mind was racing trying to make sense of everything Devon just told him. It wasn't true. It couldn't be. Was his father capable of something like that?

Yes, thought JR. His father was capable of such a thing. He always hated the man for the way he treated people. He hated him even more for the way he tried to ruin his life. JR remembered how he always asked him to bring his friends around then give them alcohol and tried to be just one of the boys. Later in school, they would laugh at the old man, leaving JR feeling humiliated. JR finished his drink, went into the kitchen, and opened a cabinet. He felt around on the top shelf and finally found what he was looking for, a small revolver. He checked to see if it had bullets in it. It did. JR went back into the living room and poured himself another drink, swallowed it in one gulp, and left the house.

JR drove to the main house and sat in the car for a minute, trying to decide if he should just walk in and kill him. No, there was a better way. JR knocked on the door, tried the handle, and walked in. His mother was walking toward the door as he walked in.

"Hello, JR, this is a nice surprise," she said.

"Hello, Mother, where's Father?" he answered angrily.

"Well, could I at least get a kiss hello?" said his mother.

"I'm sorry," he said as he gave her a small kiss in the cheek.

"Where's Father," he asked again.

"I believe he's in his study as usual," she replied. "Why, what's wrong?"

"Nothing to concern yourself with, Mother. This is between him and me," said JR as he walked to the study with his mother trailing behind. JR didn't knock; he simply opened the door and stood in front of his father.

"Have we forgotten our manners, boy? In a civilized society, it is proper to knock before entering a room with a closed door. The door being closed for a reason," said his father.

"What would you know about a civilized society?" replied JR.

"What the hell do you want, JR?" JR took the gun from his belt and pointed it at him. JR's mother yelled at him and asked him what he was doing and begged him to put the gun away.

"Sorry, Mother, can't do that. I want some information from this hypocrite, and I think this may be the only way to get it. And don't think for a minute, Father, that I won't use it. I've got nothing left to live for, so killing you would be my pleasure."

13

"Do you know about Daddy's dirty little secrets, Mother?" asked JR.

"Which one?" asked his mother.

"I want to hear about the time you raped Carolyn Taylor, but you probably knew her as Carolyn Kenmore. She was seventeen and came to pick up a check for the school. When she spurned your advances, you raped her. Tell me how that went, Father?"

"I don't know what you're talking about. Now get out!" yelled his father angrily.

"Sure, you do, Father. Just think about it awhile. I finally find someone who loves me for who I am, someone I can love, and now I find out she's my half sister. So tell me about the rape, big man. No wonder you always wanted me to bring my friends home. It was so you could hit on them, right, Father?"

"I don't know what you're talking about. Now I said to get out."

"No can do," said JR as he cocked the gun and aimed it directly at his father's head.

"Put that thing away. It's not a toy, you damn fool," said his father.

"Oh, I'm well aware of that, Father. It's going to blow a nice big hole in your head," answered JR. "Now tell me what I want to know."

"JR, please put the gun away. He isn't worth ruining your life over," said his mother. "I learned that long ago. Why do you think I kicked him out of my bedroom twenty years ago? I knew what he was doing but didn't have the courage to do anything about it then. I was so worried about keeping the Ledger name free of gossip that I forgot all the young girls he hurt. Well, I finally got the courage to do something about it. I'm leaving tomorrow. I bought a condo in Florida near my sister, and I won't be coming back. I wish I had the courage years ago. I knew what he was doing. The parade of young girls in here weekly, some of them crying as they left. I can only imagine what was going on behind this door. I was such a fool then, JR. I'm sorry."

"Well, Father, looks like you're going to be all alone. You're old and fat, so I don't think we have to worry about you picking up any young girls now. You're pitiful. That's what you are, pitiful, and I couldn't hate you more."

"Don't shoot the perverted bastard, JR," said his mother. "Just leave the gun on the desk, and maybe he'll use it on himself, or hit him where it will hurt the most. Go after his money. Yes, that's a good idea, JR. Have him draw up another will. I'd like to have a few acres of land to put a house on for when I come home for a few months in the summer. Something at the base of the mountain, I should think. Yes, that would be a wonderful place for a second home. Don't you think? And money, JR. Don't forget to leave me a lot of money. I earned every bit of it. Well, I have to go and finish packing, dear," she said as she walked to him and kissed him on the cheek. "Take care of yourself, JR. I know I didn't say it often enough, but I do love you, my dear." And she was gone.

"Well, you damn good and happy now, JR? Get what you came for?" asked his father. "Your mother's been just as big a disappointment as you are. Don't worry. She'll be back when she runs out of money. Just you wait and see."

"You may be right, Father, but I don't think so," replied JR. JR took a seat and just stared at his father. It would be really easy to kill this man. He had to work hard to keep his anger under control. His mother was right about one thing. He wasn't worth going to prison for, but it would give him such satisfaction.

"Now, Father, I think we have some business to do," said JR.

"What the hell you talking about, boy?" replied his father.

"You call me boy one more time, and I swear I'll make you eat this gun," answered JR as he rose from his chair and walked to his father, holding the gun out straight and aiming it at his face. When the gun touched his father between his eyes, JR told him to call him boy just one more time and it would be the last thing he ever said.

"All right, JR," said his father, realizing for the first time that his son might indeed pull the trigger.

JR sat back down and told his father to take out a pad of paper and a pen.

"What the hell for?" exclaimed his father.

"One, because I said so, and two, because we are going to make some changes to your will. Money is the only thing you ever cared about, so we are going to see that it goes to the right people after you blow your head off."

"Don't be ridiculous, JR. I've no intentions of committing suicide. I wouldn't give you the satisfaction," said his father.

"Well then, maybe I could hope for a heart attack. Oh no, that would mean you had a heart, and we both know that can't be true. Pick up your pen, Father, and write what I tell you. Now!" yelled JR. His father got a pad of paper out and picked up his pen, waiting for further instructions from his son.

"This will be dated today. Put in today's date, Dad, is my last will and testament. It makes all previous wills and codicils null and void, and anything written after this date to be also null and void due to my diminished mental capacity, and I hereby appoint my son, JR, to handle all my affairs as of this date," said JR.

"Holy Christ, JR! What the hell do you think you're doing? I'm not writing this," cried his father.

"Oh, but you are, Father. I have names and dates, and I'm sure everyone involved would rather not see their names in the headlines with yours, but then again, maybe I'm wrong. A lawsuit from each of the families might be a better way to go. What do you think?" With his face getting redder and sweat rolling down his forehead, Ledger Senior screamed at his son.

"I'll see you rot in hell for this, JR!"

"You can try, Father. Now let's get back to what we were doing. Why don't we take care of the little people first. How they managed to stay with you all these years is beyond me," said JR.

"It's something you'll never understand. It's called loyalty. Something I never got from you, you ungrateful son of a bitch!"

screamed his father as he got up to pour himself a drink. He took the glass and the bottle with him as he returned to his seat behind the large desk.

"Sticks and stones, Father. Sticks and stones," JR repeated, having way too much fun.

"Now where were we? To my faithful friend Carl Barnes who bred the finest foxhounds anywhere, I leave fifty thousand dollars. To my wonderful housekeeper and cook May Davis, I leave fifty thousand dollars. To any employee who has worked for me for over five years, I leave twenty thousand dollars. And to any of them who have worked under five years, I leave them ten thousand dollars. For my darling Eunice, a better wife no man has ever had, I leave the main house with all the land around it, approximately ten acres and another six acres of land at the bottom of the mountain to be chosen by JR now and properly surveyed. The fruit farm, of course, I leave to my son, JR, with the adjacent house. The horse barn and clubhouse with fifty acres of land adjacent to it, I leave to Miss Devon Taylor. All stocks, bonds, and other assets cashed in and after my lawyer takes his cut, the rest divided into three equal shares, and go to my wife, Eunice; my son, JR; and Miss Devon Taylor or Mrs., if she should marry before my demise. The land used for the foxhound chases, approximately one thousand acres, again to be surveyed and approved by my son, JR, to be donated to The Nature Conservancy with the promise that it will always remain undeveloped and kept in its wild pristine condition. You get all that, Father, or do I have to repeat it?" asked JR.

"I've got it, you dumb bastard," replied his father.

"Sticks and stones, Father," answered JR. "Now I want you to pick up the phone and tell your lawyer to come right over. You need something taken care of right away, and we all know how he jumps whenever you speak, so it shouldn't be a problem for him. Now we just sit and wait until he gets here, and just a reminder, Father. Let's not let him know you are being forced to rewrite your will. I think we should encourage him to think that you're doing it out of the goodness of your heart and concerns for your failing health and mental instability. I'm sure he will understand as he sees you slurring your words. Have another drink, Father. This could take a while," said JR. How easy it would be to just stand behind him and wrap something around his neck and squeeze the life out of him, thought JR to himself. Better yet, to use his hands and feel the life slipping out of his father's body. A bullet would be too good for him, killing him too fast, and JR wanted him to suffer. Yes, a long, slow, agonizing death was what he wished for his father. JR thought about the years in front of him and how he would get through them without Devon. His years would be long and empty. He wouldn't hear her laugh or watch her eyes light up when she spoke. He would never again run his fingers through her hair or see that perfect body. He would never feel accepted for who he was and would never let anyone else see the side of him that she loved. His plan for a perfect life with Devon was gone. Gone, gone, gone.

Gone with the utterance of just a few words: "I'm your half sister." The doorbell rang, jolting JR out of his thoughts. He got up to get it before May came running out of the kitchen. As he closed the door, May was coming toward them.

"It's okay, May. Father and Mr. Fleming and I have some work to do. We won't be needing anything," he told her.

"Are you sure? Your father usually has coffee now," she said.

"If we should want coffee later, I'll call you," replied JR softly.

"Okay then. Good night, Mr. Ledger," she said.

"Good night, May." JR followed his father's lawyer into the study.

"Evening, Russell," said Fleming. "What's so important it couldn't wait until tomorrow? JR, I'll have a little scotch and water," he said. He always treated JR as if he were a servant in the house; probably because that was how his father always treated him. This time it would be different. JR sat back down in the chair next to the desk. Fleming put his briefcase down on the floor, gave JR a rather nasty look, and went to the bar to pour himself a drink. "

JR, you forget how to take care of company?" he said. JR turned his head and looked at his father.

"We don't think of Thomas as company, do we, Father? He spends more time with you than I do. I figured he was family."

"Don't get impertinent, JR," answered his father. "Thomas is doing us a favor coming out here this late. Sorry, Thomas, I didn't want to call you out so late, but there's something that needs to be done, and I need you to put your signature and seal on it."

"Legal business at this hour? Surely it could have waited till morning," replied Fleming.

"I'm afraid it couldn't wait, Thomas. You see, Father has been feeling out of sorts lately. Some chest pains off and on, and then there's the awful forgetfulness. He might be showing early signs of Alzheimer's, so this needed to be done now while he has a clear head. I hope you understand," spoke JR.

"What are you going on about, JR? Your father is fine. He hasn't mentioned any chest pains to me, and I see him almost every day," added Fleming.

"Now you see how thoughtful Father is," said JR, trying to hold back a laugh. "He just didn't want to burden you with this."

"Russell, you feeling poorly? Have you been to the doctor's? Don't let this linger. The quicker you get some test done, the better. You don't want to be out riding and have a damn heart attack, do you?"

"I'm fine," said Russell. "I don't plan to die yet. That would make JR here too happy."

"Father, what a cruel thing to say," said JR. "What would I do without your pleasant company?"

"All right, you two, now just what are we doing?" asked Fleming.

JR spoke first. "Father has drawn up a new will, and we need you to witness it and put your magic seal on it." This time, JR couldn't hold back a small laugh, which made his father glare at him as if he were dead. No one held Russell Ledger hostage like this, no one.

"I still don't see why it couldn't have waited, but let's have a look," said Fleming. "Seems pretty straightforward, Russell, but who is this Devon Taylor, if I might ask? I've never heard of her before." But before Russell Sr. could answer, JR spoke up.

"Father's slightly embarrassed, Thomas, and has never told anyone about her, but now with his declining memory, he thought it was time to take care of this. You see, some years ago, Father had a little—now how should we put this? Well, let's just say Father had a small relationship with a woman that resulted in her giving birth to a daughter. Father has just recently become aware of the child and feels he needs to do the right thing by her even though the mother has never asked Father for anything. Father is a man of conscience, wouldn't you say, Thomas, and believes this is just a small token for the mistake he made many years ago, and since he was married to my mother at the time, well, you see the predicament he was in. Mother would have made his life a living hell. We all know how she can be. Don't we, Thomas?"

"Yes, I'm afraid we do," said Fleming. "Just how old is this girl, Russell?" Again it was JR who spoke first. "She is twenty-one, Thomas, and just finished college. She is hoping to purchase Mrs. Ogden's flower shop one day and has plans to open a no-kill animal rescue. Now isn't that ironic? Father here who would kill just about anything, and his daughter trying to save them."

"That's quite enough, JR, or I swear I'll—"

"You'll what, Father? Kill me too? Now what a terrible thing to say, and with a man who must uphold the law. That was cruel, Father. Wouldn't you say, Thomas?"

"I have no intentions of getting into a pissing match with you two. Now let's focus on the matter at hand so I can go home and have my dinner," answered Fleming. "Are you sure this is the way you want it?" asked Fleming, looking over the will. "No changes?"

"It's exactly the way it should be, Thomas. I helped him myself," said JR.

"All right then. Are you sure you don't want me to get it typed up tomorrow?" said Fleming.

"Let's just sign it now. I want it behind me as soon as possible," replied JR's father, stopping to wipe the sweat off his brow.

"Russell, just sign here. JR, you can sign here, and we still need a witness," said Fleming.

"I'll just get May. I don't think she has retired yet," answered JR. He ran off to get the housekeeper and was back in no time, for May was sitting in the kitchen, waiting for them to order coffee.

"Father needs you for a few minutes, May, then you can retire. I doubt if he will want his coffee. He and Mr. Fleming are having drinks." May followed JR into the study and was told by Mr. Fleming where to put her signature. When she was finished, she asked if anyone would like her to get them coffee.

"Thank you for your assistance, May. I don't think we will have coffee tonight. You may retire for the evening," said Russell Sr. Of all the people that worked for him, May was the only one he never got crossed with. He treated her with respect; more so than his mother ever received, which made JR always suspect that there must have been something more between them. After May left the room, Thomas signed the will and affixed a seal to it, which was just a fancy thing notaries used to prove the document was genuine. When everything was completed, JR stood up and asked for the piece of paper they had just all signed. Both men looked surprised. Fleming said it was customary for him to keep hold of it, but JR insisted that this time, he was holding it and gave no reason. Since Russell never said a word, Fleming assumed it was what he wanted. He packed up his briefcase and told Russell that he should get that checkup and not wait since he was feeling that poorly. Russell assured him that he would and said good night. JR was about to walk Fleming out to the door, but he insisted he could let himself out.

"You take care of your father, JR," said Fleming. "I know you two have knocked heads in the past, but if his health is indeed failing, then he will need you to take care of things. I don't like the way he behaved. He was so quiet tonight, JR. You get him to a doctor, understand?"

"I'll take care of it. Don't you worry, Thomas," replied JR. JR waited for Fleming to leave the house then poured himself a drink and refilled his father's.

"That went rather well, don't you think, Father?" said JR.

"I hope you burn in hell for this, JR!" yelled his father.

"I probably will, Father, right along with you. Now here, let me freshen your drink." Before he could pour more liquor into the glass, Russell picked it up and threw it at JR. It missed by a mile, which caused Russell to scream at JR to get out of the house, but JR just walked to the bar and got another glass, filled it, and placed it in front of his father.

"You want to try that again, Father? You may get lucky this time," said JR as he plopped into the chair. His father glared at him with such hatred in his eyes and every vein in his neck bulging and quickly downed his drink. JR passively got up and refilled it, just as his mother walked into the room.

"Mother, all packed?" he said.

"Yes, dear, all packed. Did I hear someone else here before?" she asked.

"Yes, Thomas Fleming took a minute to stop by and say hello," he replied.

"Oh, sorry I missed him," she said.

"Would you like a drink, Mother? Father and I are just catching up on all the things I need to take care of in case he loses his mental capabilities." JR laughed.

"Well, that shouldn't take long," snipped his mother. "It will be a favor to all of us, watching him dribble his soup that some nurse's aide is trying to feed him. Oh, now that was harsh, wasn't it? I think I will have that drink after all, JR, to celebrate my freedom.

"Father thinks I will burn in hell, Mother. What do you think?"

"Don't worry, JR. Next to your father, you are a saint, so if anyone burns in hell, it will certainly be him." Eunice raised her glass.

"A toast." JR raised his glass with her. "A toast for freedom, of ridding ourselves of the lies, the cheating, the disrespect, the ugliness I've had to endure. I deserve a good life, and by God, I mean to have it." She and JR touched their glasses and both repeated, "A toast for freedom." Then Eunice put down her glass and kissed JR good night and goodbye. As JR walked his mother to the stairway, he told her the new will was made, and she would be well taken care of, and he also made sure she got those few acres she wanted at the base of the mountain. His mother kissed him again for a job well done and climbed the stairs for the last time. Before he left for the evening, JR placed the bottle of scotch closer to his father and thanked him for an entertaining and productive evening.

JR still had one thing to do. He knew it was late, but he hoped Devon's father was still up. As he got to the lodge, he began to shake. Giving himself a few minutes to calm down, he entered the lodge, hoping that he wouldn't see Mrs. Taylor or Devon. Luckily, he found him alone and asked to speak to him in private. JR explained about the new will his father had drawn up this evening after JR confronted him about his raping Carolyn. Warren told him they didn't want Ledgers' money, but JR convinced him that it could make all Devon's dreams come true, and that was what he wanted for her.

"You can't be a part of her life, JR," said Mr. Taylor.

"I know."

"She has to move on without you, so please, if you care for her, stay away," said her father sadly.

"I'll always love her, and I'll always be there for her if she ever needs a shoulder to cry on, but I promise I will never, ever take advantage of her. I promise you. I wouldn't tell your wife anything about the will. I know she wouldn't want anything to do with my father, and I can't blame her, but it's for Devon." Devon's father agreed he would keep the secret and told JR he trusted him to keep his word. JR left. As he got into his car and took one last look back at the lodge, he thought to himself that he did a good thing tonight. This day cost him everything, and he cried as he slowly drove away alone again.

14

Devon got up at nine and went down to breakfast; she grabbed a bowl of cereal with fruit and went to sit outside. Soon she was joined by her mother.

"Morning, honey," said her mom. "Sleep well?"

"Fine," answered Devon. Actually she didn't sleep at all. The pain was still too real. She waited for her mother to say something about the truth she was finally told, but her mother said nothing.

"Do you think you have enough clothes for a while, or would you like to go to Albany to shop some more?" said her mother.

"I have enough, but if you want to shop for yourself, I'd be happy to go along," she answered.

"No, I really don't need anything. Just trying to grab every second I can with you before you leave."

"I love you too, Mom, but I'll be home every other weekend, and we still have, what, ten days before I leave," said Devon.

"I know. I'm just being foolish. My baby bird is about to take off, and I miss her already."

Devon put her bowl down and hugged her mother. "I won't fly far. I promise."

"So what do you have planned for the rest of your vacation?" asked her mother.

"Not really sure. The only thing I have to do is pick up the flowers on Monday, but the rest of my time is free. I guess I'll just help out at the lodge.

"That doesn't sound like much of a vacation, even though your father and I love you helping around the lodge," said her mother. "Not much else to do really. Rory's in New Paltz, but her boyfriend is coming up for a long weekend, and I really don't want to call Sarah. She won't go anywhere without the creep."

"That's too bad. You used to be such good friends."

"Yeah, I know. Sarah was my best friend until she got caught up by him. I even heard that she may be doing drugs with him. I just don't understand why she doesn't see him for what he is," exclaimed Devon.

"Love does strange things. It often blinds us, so we really don't see clearly," she said. Devon wondered if that remark was aimed at her.

"I guess so. So what do you think I should do for the rest of my vacation?" Devon asked.

"Why don't you go up to Lake George. Don't you still have a friend there, Jean or Jane something?"

"Wow, I haven't spoken to Jane for some time. I think it was when we finished our second year of school. I have no idea what she's doing now."

"Well, call and find out, unless you really like scrubbing pots. We have a full house, and I think the kitchen could use some help."

"You know, I think I'll call my friend Jane and see what she's up to," declared Devon as she got up to bring her bowl back to the kitchen but stopped to give her mother a kiss. "Thanks, Mom. I love you." Devon could tell that her mother must have been going through hell with the burden she had been carrying, and she hoped it wouldn't affect her health. The dark circles under her eyes told Devon that she hadn't slept. *Please,* she prayed, *keep her all right while I'm away.*

Devon called Jane and was invited to come up and spend a few days. She told Jane she could come up to Lake George on Wednesday because she had to pick up the flowers in New York on Monday and work in the shop on Tuesday, but she could take the rest of the week off. She had to leave on Saturday because Sunday, her parents needed her at the lodge. There was a wedding there, and Devon had to do the flowers, and then she would be picking up the flowers again on Monday, and it would be her last day working in the shop until she got done with grooming school.

Devon drove to Lake George to Jane's house. She was so surprised by the size of the house her friend lived in. She always assumed that because Jane had been going to the community college that her parents didn't have much money. Boy was she wrong. Jane ran to greet her, and both girls hugged and jumped up and down, so happy to be seeing each other after a year. They couldn't wait to find out what each of them had been doing. Jane's mother came out of the house to greet Devon and told Jane to help Devon with her things and to put them in the room next to hers then come out on the veranda as lunch was being served. Jane and Devon grabbed the bags, ran upstairs, and threw the things into the room, then sat on the bed trying to catch up on everything from the past year. Devon finally said that they should go down to lunch before they got into trouble on the first day. Jane was like a breath of fresh air; just what Devon needed.

Jane introduced her parents to Devon, and Devon was bubbling over with joy when she learned that Jane's father was a veterinarian. For a second she had forgotten everyone else and began asking him every question she could think of. Then she stopped in midsentence, totally embarrassed and apologized for her rudeness. Jane's parents began to laugh and accepted her apology. Mr. Fredrickson remarked that Jane had told them how devoted she was to animals and about her desire to own her own pet store and shelter one day, and now listening to her speaking so intensely about her plans, they knew things hadn't changed.

"Please, Devon," said Mr. Fredrickson, "if I may ask, why didn't you want to become a vet? You certainly have the passion, and as Jane told us, you were the smartest in your classes."

"I really don't have an answer, Mr. Fredrickson. It's strange that I never considered it. I just knew I was meant to be involved with and save and love as many animals as I could and as soon as I could. Maybe subconsciously I thought becoming a vet would take too long. I really don't know."

"Devon, dear, I'm sure Jane would like a little of your time while you're here, and you and Geoffrey can talk animals all you want, but right now, let's have a pleasant lunch and get caught up. How are your parents, dear?" asked Mrs. Fredrickson. "As I remember, they owned a lodge in the Catskills."

"Yes, they do," answered Devon. "They're fine, and the lodge is doing great. It's filled to capacity right through Labor Day. Dad made a lot of improvements over the last few years, both indoors and out, and things have really improved. The lodge never had central air, so Dad had that installed, and we now have a real chef in the kitchen, so the food has been fantastic. A new pool was put in and a wading pool for kids and the pond enlarged and stocked for anyone who wants to fish."

"Well, I'd say that is quite an ambitious undertaking," said Mr. Fredrickson. "I'm glad they are doing so well."

"Yes, that is such an undertaking," said Mrs. Fredrickson. "I imagine they need no help falling asleep at night."

"No, they work pretty long hours, but they love it," replied Devon. "I can't imagine them doing anything else. Sometimes I feel guilty not helping as much as I should, but with school and the flower shop and now grooming school, I just don't have the time."

"You must tell us all about your plans," said Mrs. Fredrickson, "but now I think Jane wants you to herself. All right, girls, you're excused. Remember dinner at seven. See you then." Before Mrs. Fredrickson could get the last word out, Jane and Devon were already running down the stairs that led to the lake. When they got to the bottom, they sat down on the grass near the lake. Jane's parents had a boathouse on the lake, and Devon could see a rather large boat inside. Devon had to wonder why Jane always projected an image of a poor girl when she was anything but. In college, Jane was one of Devon's best friends and had her stay over many times at the lodge. Jane never mentioned her parents, which Devon thought was unusual, and now having met them, she couldn't help but wonder again. They seemed wonderful.

The two girls lay back on the grass and stared up at the clouds. Neither spoke for a few minutes, then both of them began to ask each other questions about what they had done since they said goodbye a year ago. Devon filled Jane in about all the people they knew from school and what they were up to now. Some of the boys had gone on to other colleges to finish their degrees, and others had enlisted in the service, some in the Army, others in the Marines. Devon couldn't remember who went where though. Jimmy Cane, one of the boys Jane was interested in and had a few dates with, had gone into the Marines. Devon was sure of that. His grades weren't high enough to get any scholarships, and his parents didn't have the money, so he enlisted. Jane hoped he wasn't sent to any war zone. She really liked him and would feel awful if he were killed. They spent the better part of the afternoon catching up, then Jane suggested a swim before dinner. The girls raced up to the house, put on their suits, and ran back down to the lake. Devon, ever the daring one, dove in first. She yelled to Jane to come in, but Jane said the water was probably too cold. Devon began to cluck like a chicken, so Jane finally dove in. They swam to a small deck anchored in the water by Jane's father. The water had been cold, and it felt good to lie in the sunshine. They lay sunning themselves when a small boat stopped near them with a few guys in it. Yelling out to Jane, who appeared to know them all, they asked if the water was cold. Jane told them to go in and find out for themselves. All three boys jumped from the boat and swam to the deck. As they clung to the sides of the deck, Jane introduced the boys to Devon. They hopped onto the deck, nearly overturning it, and asked the girls what they were doing later. Jane told them dinner at seven as usual, but they had no plans after that. One of the boys suggested they take Devon for a little sightseeing downtown, but Jane said they would have to clear it with her parents. As all the boys were known to Jane, she promised to call one of them if her parents said it was okay; and with that, they swam back to the boat, which had floated farther down the lake. They could hear each of them complaining to the other why someone didn't throw out the anchor. Jane and Devon got a good laugh watching them swim to catch the moving boat. The two of them decided they had enough sunbathing, especially since Devon hadn't thought to put any sunscreen on, and the last thing she wanted was to be beet red on her first day.

They found Jane's mother on the veranda, and Jane told her how Kenny, Bobby, and Chase had stopped by with the boat and invited them out. They wanted to show Devon downtown Lake George since she had never been there before. Her mother was hesitant but gave in because she knew all the boys and their families, most of which were extremely wealthy, and all had homes on the lake. Jane called Chase and said they could go but not until at least nine, which he said was fine. Dinner with the Fredricksons was a lot more formal than at the lodge. Cut crystal glasses, fine china, and a complete set of dinnerware. Devon hoped she could remember which piece of cutlery to use at each course. Dinner seemed to go on forever, but eventually they were finished, and the girls ran up to freshen up with Jane's mother calling to them that she wanted them home by twelve.

Chase, Kenny, and Bobby were waiting outside in Chase's silver convertible, and everyone jockeyed around to see who would be sitting by Devon. It ended up with Kenny, Bobby, and Devon in the backseat; and Chase and Jane in the front. Chase pulled away from the house a little too fast and sent small stones scattering in the driveway. Chase remarked that he would probably catch hell from Jane's dad for that one, and Jane agreed. They rode around a part of the lake then went down into the town where all the tourists were. The boys joked that they rarely came down here because it was a place for the tourist, but because Devon had never been here before, they made an exception for her. They walked the streets for a while and asked if Devon had had enough. When she said she did, the guys drove to the nearest store for beer. Then they drove to the private beach at Chase's home. The guys lit a small fire and handed Jane and Devon each a beer. The night proved to be a lot of fun with the guys singing their favorite songs for Devon. It was over so quickly, and they got home right at midnight. Mrs. Fredrickson was still up, no doubt waiting for the girls. Devon was used to it. Here she was, twenty-one, and her parents still waited up for her, so it didn't bother her at all, but Jane had a much different reaction.

"You didn't have to wait up for us, you know. I know what twelve o'clock means. I wish you would stop treating me like a child," said Jane and ran up the stairs to her room.

"Did you have a pleasant evening, Devon?" she asked, trying not to cause a scene with Jane while Devon was standing there.

"Yes, I did. Jane's friends gave me a wonderful tour of the town and part of the lake, and then we went to Chase's house to sit on the beach. It was getting chilly, so the boys lit a fire. They were so funny, singing us songs. It was really fun," answered Devon.

"I'm so glad. Please excuse Jane for her little outburst," said Mrs. Fredrickson.

"It's no problem. I'm used to having my parents wait up for me. Usually my mom and I talk all about my dates while I'm getting ready for bed," replied Devon.

"How nice for you. I'm afraid Jane and I don't share the same closeness as you and your mother. I've tried but not very successfully. Well, good night, dear," said Mrs. Fredrickson. Devon walked upstairs and knocked softly on Jane's door. Jane opened the door and let Devon in.

"What's with all the drama downstairs?" asked Devon. "It's so much easier to just say hello and good night than go through what you just did. What's really going on, Jane?"

"I'm sorry, but it's aggravating having her treat me like a child," answered Jane.

"She's not treating you like a child. My parents still wait up for me to come home. They just need to know that you're okay, that's all. It's a parent thing," said Devon.

"No, it's become unbearable since Michael died," cried Jane as she turned her face into her pillow and sobbed.

"Jane, please, talk to me. Who's Michael?" Jane sat up, her eyes all red from crying, and pulled the pillow onto her lap. She wiped her face with the back of her hand. Devon always kept a tissue in her pocket and offered her one. Jane managed to pull herself together and wiped her face, but she still sobbed. Devon moved closer and took her hand.

"Please, Jane," she asked. "Tell me what's wrong."

"Michael was my brother, my older brother. He was three years older than I was. I adored him. He was such a great brother, and he was the golden boy, the one my parents' dreams hung on. He was tall, handsome, smart, and so charismatic. Everyone loved Michael. I loved him so much. At school all the girls wanted to be with me in case Michael stopped by to talk to me. Then they would all giggle and scream because they got so close to him. It was really funny. He would just do it for fun, and we would talk and laugh about it when we got home. He was so special. He knew he had it all, but that didn't make him stuck-up or anything. He was just so cool. He was the best brother in the world." Jane started crying again and put the pillow over her face to muffle the sound she made. The last thing she needed was for her mother to hear her. Devon tried to be patient and let Jane cry.

"I know my parents love me, but it was different before. Michael was always the center of attention, and I was just another member of the family. I didn't mind, really, because Michael and I had our own thing going that didn't include our parents. Wherever he went, he always brought me back something even if it was just a candy bar. Mom was always on me about eating sweets. She didn't want to see me gain any weight. I had to be pencil thin in her world or I wouldn't be attractive. I was just a few weeks from graduating from high school, and my eighteenth birthday was at the end of May. Michael was in his second year at Cornell, following in Dad's shoes to become a vet. Mom went overboard as usual and hired one of the paddle boats that went around the lake, complete with a band and midafternoon buffet. She never could just have a cake and family like everyone else. It always had to be grander than grand. Michael was supposed to come home on Friday night after his last class, and we waited and waited, but he never showed up. Dad called his room, and his roommate said that Michael left around four that afternoon. Mother became hysterical afraid that something had happened to him, and she was right. The chief of police who was a good friend of my dad's showed up and said that there had been an accident. Michael must have taken some of the back roads over the mountain and, because it was so foggy that night, failed to make a curve and ran off the road, hitting a tree. He was killed instantly. I remember we all just stood there without moving or saying anything. Chief Fletcher somehow managed to get us all into the living room and sitting down. When he spoke again to say how sorry he was, Mother stood up and screamed at him, calling him a liar and telling him how cruel he was to make up such a story. She started to hit the chief on his chest before Dad grabbed her. Then she just lost it, throwing herself on the floor and screaming Michael's name. I remember Dad asked the chief to call our family doctor. It was so terrible watching her go through that. Dad was crying, but he managed to keep it together. I don't know when I left them and went to my room. I just knew I had to get away from everyone. I didn't cry. I don't think I really understood what the chief had just told us. I remember I felt cold and numb. I crawled into my bed and covered my head with the blankets. I thought when I got up things would be all right. I must have fallen asleep. I don't know for how long, but the next thing I remember was Mrs. Stillman pulling the blankets down and talking to me. She asked me how I was, and I told her I didn't know that I had an awful dream about Michael being killed. She sat on the bed and took me in her arms and told me that it wasn't a dream. Michael was dead. I cried while she held me, then she told me to go back to sleep and asked me if I needed anything to help me sleep. I thought I was still in my dream and told her no, that I would be okay. When I awoke, it was my birthday, and I remembered the party and Michael. I ran down the stairs screaming where's Michael. He promised he would come to the party, and that's when my father grabbed me and held me tight and said Michael was dead. The house was full of people, friends of Mom and Dad's. They had food set up in the dining room, and some were greeting other people as they arrived. It was so unreal. The food that was going to be served for my birthday celebration was now being used to feed the people that came for Michael. Mother was in her room, heavily sedated. I was told not to bother her. I remember going back up to my room, and a few of my girlfriends and Warren and Bobby came to sit with me. They all left after a while, and I was alone again. Michael's funeral was a blur. I remembered being shuffled from person to person then told to sit here or there, eat or don't eat. I was just forgotten and pushed into a corner, then I was told to go to my room. I don't know how long I remained in my room before someone finally remembered me. I don't think I had anything to eat for two days, not that I could anyway, but I was told I needed to eat or become ill, and the doctor didn't want two patients on his hands. I knew they meant my mother because I hadn't seen her since the night the chief came to the house. For the next few weeks, people were in and out. I was forced to go to school every day so I would be able to graduate, and

I did. Just Dad was there. The next few weeks were the same, people coming and going. Dad went back to work, and Mother was still in her room. When she finally started coming down for meals, she would stare at me so intensely. I could feel her eyes boring through me. I knew what she was thinking as she looked at me. Why wasn't it you instead of Michael? It was as if I could hear her thoughts. I finally stopped eating at the same time as her, and Dad knew why, but he couldn't do anything. He just let me do what I had to. By the end of July, I knew I had to get away. I remembered this lady who was the mother of one of mom's friends. She lived in Greenport, and I knew Columbia Greene Community College was there, so I called her. She knew all about Michael's death and was just so sweet and understanding. I asked if she knew if anyone was renting out rooms to college students since there were no dorms. She spoke up right away and said I would live with her, and she wouldn't take no for an answer. I was thrilled. I contacted the school and got accepted and was told that classes started in just a few weeks. I waited for Dad and told him my plans. At first he balked at the idea, but considering the atmosphere around the house, he told me to go. I packed, took some money out of the bank, and kissed him goodbye. I never saw my mother. I just left. Dad wanted me home for Christmas. I said I could only stay a day or two because I had some extra work to finish. I shouldn't have bothered to go home. She was the same. Mother and Father had a huge fight about the way she was treating me, so I left the day after Christmas. A memorial for Michael was held and the stone placed at his grave. I came home for that but left soon after, and I really haven't had much to do with her until last summer. Dad wanted me home to discuss where I would go next year. We decided on Syracuse. I was very good in science and decided I wanted to become a biology teacher. Dad had hoped that I would go to Cornell and go to vets school, but I told him I couldn't. It wasn't something I thought I could do. So we agreed on Syracuse, and that's where I went last year. I only came home this summer because Dad insisted that Mother and I needed some time together to work out our problems. What problems, I told him. As far as mother was concerned, it should have been me instead of Michael that was killed in that auto accident. He told me she was better and to please try to get along with her. I have. Every day I try, but most of the time, she just glares at me, and when she isn't glaring, she's smothering me. Where are you going? Who are you going with? When will you be home? What time exactly? She's been driving me crazy. I can't stand it. If I take the car, she really loses it."

"I'm really sorry for everything you've been through. I can't imagine what it must have been like. Not having a sibling, I wouldn't know, but try to look at it from her side. She already lost one child. She can't lose another," said Devon.

"If that was what it was, I would try harder, but she isn't concerned about losing me. She already lost her only child, so why should I care?" answered Jane.

"I'm sorry you feel that way, Jane. I think you and your mother are missing out on a lot of good times, but like I said, I can't offer advice because I don't know what you're feeling," replied Devon.

"I don't even know what I'm feeling. All I know is that I can't wait for school to start. I've already decided to go back to Syracuse early. Actually I'm leaving shortly after you go back to Catskill. Dad's not thrilled. He keeps hoping Mom and I will have some kind of a breakthrough and get passed all this, but I don't ever see it happening," said Jane sadly. "Look, I'm rather tired. Can we pick this up later?"

"Sure, Jane, I'll talk to you tomorrow. Any specific time we have to be down for breakfast?" asked Devon.

"There's a time for everything, Devon. Breakfast is anywhere between eight and nine so Father can have something before he leaves for the day. If it's after nine, you fend for yourself in the kitchen, Mother's rules," replied Jane sarcastically.

"Okay, I'll see you tomorrow, good night," said Devon as she left for her room, yawning. Devon looked at her watch and realized that the two of them had been talking for over two hours. She felt so sad for Jane. She couldn't imagine what it would be like not to have her mother to speak with. Her mom was what kept her going.

15

DEVON CALLED HOME IN the morning; she needed to hear her mom's voice after the all-night session with Jane. Despite the last few days and the confession her mom told her, she sounded good, which made Devon feel better. Devon said she might be home a little earlier than planned because this was not a very happy house. Her mother reminded her that Jane might need her to be there for her if things were that bad. Devon agreed and told her mother how lucky she was to have her in her life. A quick I love you and goodbye. Devon met Jane coming out of her bedroom.

"I think we may have missed breakfast. How about going into town to the diner?" she asked Jane.

"Yeah, I'd like that," replied Jane. "Let's see if we can sneak out."

"No," said Devon firmly, "I don't sneak. We'll just inform her we are going out to breakfast, and if you're afraid to face her, I'll tell her." Devon found Mrs. Fredrickson still at the table, sipping coffee and reading a magazine and didn't hear Devon approaching.

"Good article," said Devon.

"Not really. I don't know where these designers get their ideas from. They seem to want to make us all look like we are wearing cloth sacks. Horrible designs for this year," replied Mrs. Fredrickson. Before she could get another word in, Devon quickly informed her that she and Jane were going into town to have breakfast and maybe do some shopping and not to wait for them for lunch, as she didn't know when they would be back. Mrs. Fredrickson looked like she was about to say something but changed her mind and looked back at the magazine.

"We'll call if we won't be back in time for dinner," added Devon and scooted out the door before Mrs. Fredrickson could reply. Jane, who had been waiting outside by her car, asked what her mother said. Devon told her she didn't say anything, and that she didn't give her time to. She just bolted out the door. Jane laughed victoriously till she started tearing up. Devon wasn't sure if they were sad tears or happy ones. They headed to the diner for breakfast and passed Chase and Kenny on the way. The boys turned around and followed the girls to the diner.

"Somebody missed breakfast time," teased Chase.

"Shut up, Chase," said Jane. "Don't you have somewhere to be?"

"Nope, I'm right where I want to be. Good morning, Devon." Chase smiled as he took the seat next to her, leaving Kenny to sit with Jane.

"So, girls, what's the plan for today?" asked Chase.

"Nothing that includes you," snapped Jane.

"Wow, somebody got up on the wrong side of the bed," he said.

"I'm sorry, Chase," said Jane. "I would just like to have a nice, quiet breakfast and talk to Devon."

"Then what?" he said.

"I don't know. Maybe some shopping. Why are you so interested anyway?" replied Jane.

"Just being neighborly. Thought we could take Devon for a boat ride around the lake. What do you say, Devon? Up for that?" said Chase.

"Yeah," she answered. "That sounds like fun. So why don't you disappear for a while and come back in an hour and we'll go. That all right with you, Jane?"

"I guess so," answered Jane.

"Okay, ladies, enjoy your breakfast, and I'll get the boat gassed up and be back in an hour," said Warren. "Come on, Kenny. Girls have to eat."

The guys left, and the girls ordered breakfast. Jane was surprised by the breakfast Devon ordered: pancakes, two scrambled eggs, bacon and toast, and coffee.

"Do you eat like that all the time?" asked Jane.

"Usually, we always have a large breakfast and a light dinner. A little backward for some people, but it works for us," replied Devon.

"If I ate like that, Mother would be all over me," said Jane.

"Why, you have the entire day to work it off?" said Devon.

"I guess so, but she still wouldn't like it. She seems to get a perverse pleasure telling me how fat I'm going to become if I eat too much," replied Jane.

"Well, your mother's not around now, so have what you want," said Devon. So Jane ordered the same thing as Devon. The girls ate leisurely, talking about nothing special, when they saw Chase and Kenny pull up.

"God, has it been an hour already?" asked Jane.

"I guess," said Devon. "Look, Jane, we don't have to go if you'd rather not. It's okay with me. I'm not crazy about Chase anyway."

"No, it's all right. You'll love the ride around the lake. It's really beautiful here," said Jane. Chase told Jane to leave her car at the diner, and they would pick it up later. Maybe they would come back for burgers or something. The four of them got into Chase's car, and Devon couldn't help but notice all the empty beer cans on the floor.

"You guys been to a party last night and forget to clean out your car?" asked Devon.

"No, it's usually that way." Chase laughed. They drove to Chase's house and walked down the hill to the beach and boathouse. Chase asked if they brought their bathing suits. Both girls did because they thought they would go to the large beach on the lake after shopping. Chase suggested they change into their suits in case they cause some waves and they get wet. Both girls went into the small cabana to change and walked back to the boys. Suddenly, Chase grabbed Devon by the wrist and tried to kiss her. She pulled away and told him to knock it off. He just laughed and downed another can of beer and threw it on the ground. The ground was littered with empty beer cans.

"Have you been drinking all morning?" asked Devon.

"Course not," answered Chase, "not all morning. Just a part of it."

Devon was really upset and told Jane she would like to go. She wasn't getting in a boat with a drunk. Chase became agitated and grabbed Devon's arm again. This time he wrestled her to the ground while trying to get the top of her bathing suit off. Devon screamed at him to stop, but Chase became angrier. He tore one of the straps to the top of her suit then tried to pull down the bottoms. Devon was screaming for him to stop, and when he didn't, she pleaded with Jane and Kenny to do something. Kenny was just laughing when Jane looked at him and told him to stop being an ass and help her with Chase. They finally managed to get Chase off Devon, and she quickly stood up, holding up the top of her suit. Chase jumped up also and laughed and went after Devon again.

"I'm warning you, Chase, stay away from me," she said.

"What's wrong with our little country mouse? Don't you want a little fun?" he said and began to move closer to her. Devon waited until he got close enough then rammed him with her knee between his legs. Chase doubled over and fell to the ground. Devon started to run, calling for Jane to follow. When they got up to the house, they weren't sure what they should do, but Devon jumped onto Chase's car. Luckily, the keys were still in the ignition. Devon asked Jane how to get back to her house. When they arrived at Jane's house, her father was there having lunch. Jane's mother came quickly to the door when she heard the girls. She asked what was wrong, and Devon and Jane began to tell her what Chase tried to do to Devon. Jane was in tears but not Devon. Her mother suggested that maybe they misunderstood Chase's intentions and overreacted. Devon showed her the strap he tore off and said in no uncertain terms that she did not misinterpret Chase's intensions. Mr. Fredrickson came into the foyer to see what the ruckus was about, and when Devon explained that Chase was drunk and tried to rape her, he was shocked. He asked if she was hurt, and she showed him her wrists and left arm that was already showing bruising. He told the girls to go up and change, and then they would discuss this further. When the girls came back downstairs, Mrs. Stillman was there, and when she saw Devon, she screamed that she wanted that girl arrested for accosting her son and stealing his car.

"I didn't steal his car. We came home to change, and we were going to pick up Jane's at the diner where we left it, and then we were going to put Chase's car back," exclaimed Devon. "As for accosting him, he got what he deserved for trying to rape me," cried Devon.

"My Chase would never behave in such a manner. You must have led him on," she replied.

Mr. Fredrickson asked Jane if what Devon had told them was true. She said it was, and that she and Kenny had to drag Chase off her, and that he was really drunk.

"Why would you go with him if he was drunk?" asked Jane's father.

"When we saw him at the diner, he wasn't, but he picked us up an hour later and seemed all right, but there were a lot of empty beer cans in the car, and at the beach, we just never thought that he was drunk until we got to the beach and saw all the empties," said Jane. "Ask Kenny. He helped me with Chase."

"Where is he now?" asked Mr. Fredrickson.

"Kenny is still at the house with Chase. The poor boy is suffering, so I'll probably have to call the doctor," cried Mrs. Stillman.

"Jane, call Kenny and tell him I want to speak to him now," said Mr. Fredrickson. Jane did as she was told and dialed Kenney. He said he would be right up. Mrs. Fredrickson suggested they all go into the living room where they would be more comfortable. She asked Mrs. Stillman, who she called Eva, if she would like anything, and she replied that she would like a dry martini. Devon noted that it was only one thirty. She sat on the couch and sipped her drink, all the while complaining how her Chase was in such pain and that she really should get home to him. The doorbell rang, and it was Kenny. Jane asked him to go into the living room. Mr. Fredrickson asked Kenny an account of the advents that had just happened down at the boathouse. Kenny looked at Mrs. Stillman and hesitated to say anything. Mr. Fredrickson asked again, raising his voice this time. Kenny looked at the floor, paused, and then finally told him of what just happened with Chase and Devon. He said Chase had been drinking all morning and said he planned to get Devon once they were at the beach; that he planned to rape the country mouse, as he called her. He told them that he and Jane pulled him off her, and that was when she kneed him. With all three stories the same, Mr. Fredrickson told Eva that Chase was clearly at fault. She stammered that it was all made-up because they were just jealous of her Chase. Kenny told her that Chase was really drinking a lot and starting in the morning now.

"Nonsense," she said.

"Your son is going to kill someone or himself driving drunk like that, and the next time, he may rape some girl," said Devon. "You need to get him some help," pleaded Devon.

"There is nothing wrong with my Chase," said Eva.

"Driving drunk will get him killed," stated Devon again. "Mrs. Fredrickson, if she is really your friend, then tell her what it's like to lose a son." And with that, Devon ran up the stairs to her room and began to pack. Nothing she could say would make any difference; these people lived in their own little world. Devon was almost finished packing when Jane knocked on the door. Devon opened it and told Jane to come in.

"So what are they going to do? Am I being arrested?" she said.

"No, of course not. They believed us, especially since Kenny backed us up," Jane replied.

"Oh, good, I could be sitting in jail if it wasn't for Kenny. I'm sorry, Jane, but if this is what the people are like here, then it's no wonder you went away. As you can see, I'm leaving now," exclaimed Devon.

"I'm really sorry, Devon. I had no idea any of this would happen," cried Jane.

"I know," replied Devon, "but these people have to get a grip on reality. Even your mother looked like she didn't believe me."

"I'm sorry about that. She and Eva go way back. She was there for Mom when Michael died," said Jane.

"I hate to predict the future, but I think your mother will be needed when Chase wraps himself around a tree," said Devon.

"Devon, you're right. I can't stay here. I'm going to pack and go back to school early. Father will understand, and as for Mother, well, I just can't be held hostage by her any longer."

"I'm sorry, Jane, but I think you're making the right choice. Get out now before it gets worse," replied Devon. The girls hugged each other, and Jane gave Devon her address at school. Devon didn't know her address yet, but that Jane could write to her at the lodge because she would be coming home every other weekend. Jane helped Devon down with her things and placed them in the car.

Devon walked back into the house and was glad that Mrs. Stillman was no longer there. She thanked Jane's parents for their hospitality. Mr. Fredrickson asked Devon to reconsider leaving, that the matter was taken care of, but Devon told him she needed to go. Jane walked her to her car and cried when she left, then went back inside and informed her parents that she was returning to college early herself. Jane's father didn't say a word, but her mother just poured herself a drink.

16

Devon ran into the lodge to find her mother and father. She quickly spotted her father and threw herself into his arms and told him how much she loved him then asked where her mother was. Devon raced to the office and into her mother's arms and told her how much she loved her too. Her father entered the office and asked what was going on and why Devon was back so early. Devon asked for something to eat, and then she would tell them everything.

Devon's father was furious when Devon told them what happened; she had all she could do to keep him from calling the police and having Chase arrested. Devon told him not to because the Stillmans were rich like everyone else that lived on the lake, and they wouldn't do anything to him. Jane had told her that the guys were always in trouble, and nothing was ever done to them. Devon's mother was horrified just thinking of what her daughter had endured, but she was home safe now, and that was all that mattered. She just couldn't let herself think of what could happen to her in New York City.

On Monday, Devon would make her first trip to New York City alone. She accompanied Mrs. Ogden a few times before and made a pretty clear map, but today, she was on her own. They picked up flowers from the many wholesale flower merchants. Devon was so excited about the trip except for the ungodly hour she had to be there; up at four to be in the city by six or seven at the latest. Mrs. Ogden always did business with the same merchants. One for regular flowers like mums, carnations, and such; and some of the others for the more exotic flowers like the orchids. This particular Monday morning, Devon would meet a man who would change her life. Devon stopped to get herself a cup of coffee and a bagel with cream cheese. She had made good time on the ride down, hitting very little traffic. Not too many cars were on the roads at four in the morning, just trucks that she let breeze by. She finally learned the best way to get down to the flower district, which covered a few blocks around Twenty-Seventh Street and Seventh Avenue. She parked the van and went into the first shop on the list, Nardell Brothers' Inc., ran by Kevin and Ray Nardell, second generation floral merchants. Their father, Raymond Senior, opened the shop over forty years ago and still came in a few days a week to make sure the flowers they were selling were of the best quality. You paid a little more, but you knew you got the best. As Devon entered the store, it wasn't the same. Normally the flowers were precisely arranged in neat rows, and most were in the large walk-in coolers, but today was different.

"Good morning, Ray," said Devon. "Doing a little remodeling?"

"Good morning, Ms. Taylor, I mean, Devon." Devon had asked the brothers to drop the formalities and call her Devon, but occasionally Ray forgot. "No, we are having problems with the refrigeration unit. Got some men on it now. Sorry for the inconvenience," he said.

"No problem. I'm a little early today, so I don't mind hanging around," she answered. Ray offered her a cup of coffee, which she gladly accepted. She tried to stay out of the way with men walking in and out.

"How long have they been working?" she asked Ray, who was holding his mug and slurping his coffee. Devon chuckled to herself, watching him bring the hot coffee to his lips and slurp some off the edge. Ray was the older brother; Devon guessed he was around sixty, and his brother, Kevin, just a year or two younger.

"Since two. I came in a little early, waiting for Kevin coming back from the airport, and I find the coolers down. So I call our man, and he comes with his crew. They should be done soon. He's a good man and got a good crew. They know their business," said Ray. "But what a mess. I'm only glad Pops decided not to come in today. He would have had a heart attack." Devon and Ray sipped their coffee for another five minutes or so when a large man approached Ray. Devon estimated he had to be at least six feet three or four, not overweight, just big. He wore a gray jumpsuit with a logo on the pocket that said "Griffin Air" and written in small letters was "Eddie." He smiled when he saw Devon; one of those ear-to-ear smiles, showing the whitest teeth. Devon smiled back as he approached them. She could see the sparkle in his soft brown eyes as he grinned. Still looking at Devon, he said to Ray that everything was fixed and working okay. The boys were just picking up their tools, and they would be out of the way in a few minutes. Ray told him to tell the men that he had put on some coffee and had fresh doughnuts, bagels, and cream cheese. As the first man walked out, Eddie relayed the message to him and told him to pass it along to the other guys. It was something the brothers always did if they had to call them out early because of some equipment failure. Eddie kept staring at Devon until Ray told him to show a little respect for one of his best customers. Devon thought it was funny and decided to say something to Ray.

"It's all right, Ray. I'm sure Mr. I'm sorry I didn't get your name," she said.

"It's Griffin, Eddie Griffin, but please call me Eddie. Everyone does, right, Ray?" Still talking to Ray but looking at Devon.

"That's right. This is Eddie. He owns the business. Eddie, this is Ms. Taylor, all the way down from the Catskills," replied Ray.

"Ms. Taylor, it's a pleasure," he said.

"Please call me Devon. Everyone does, right, Ray?" she said laughingly.

"Oh, and funny too. You didn't tell me that, Ray," he said jokingly.

"What am I, a mind reader now?" he answered. "If I leave you alone with her, no funny business, understand? Devon, please excuse me for just a moment. I want to make sure the guys get some food before they go. I'll be right back, and you behave," he said as he looked at Eddie.

"I promise I'll be good, Dad," he said as Ray walked away. "So, Ms. Taylor, the Catskills, nice place."

"Please call me Devon."

"So, Devon, the Catskills, nice place," he said as he tried to keep from laughing. "I'm sorry. Don't mind me. I tend to get a little silly when I don't get enough sleep. We had a job before Ray called, and I've been up now for about twenty-four hours," he said as he checked his watch.

"It's all right. I get that way too, but now that you're finished here, you can go home, jump into bed, and catch up on some much-needed sleep," said Devon.

"If only I could," he said. "We still have another job to take care of, but it's just a small job, so I should be done by noon. That's if nothing else goes wrong. So you come down every Monday for flowers?"

"I've just started to. Mrs. Ogden, the woman who owns the shop I work in, has been ill, and I volunteered to make the run for her," answered Devon.

"You like working in the shop?"

"I do," she answered, "but it's only part-time. I also work in the lodge, and I just finished college."

"Boy, busy girl. Doesn't leave much time for fun, does it?"

"I manage to squeeze in a little now and then. My parents own the lodge, and I really don't do much unless they get a full house, but I do all the flower arrangements, and that can take some time, especially when we change seasons. But I love it, so it really doesn't seem like work."

"What were you going to college for?" asked Eddie.

"I took business management and accounting," answered Devon.

"Ambitious."

"Some could say that. I have a plan for most of my life, and right now, I'm working on the foundation," she replied.

"Boy, I'd like to hear that plan," said Eddie. "Any chance we could have breakfast next time you come down, or doesn't your plan allow you to eat?"

"My plan is very flexible, and it does allow me a few minutes now and then to eat something," she said.

"Is that a yes for breakfast?" he said.

"I really don't have much time. I have to get the flowers back to the shop," said Devon.

"Come on," replied Eddie. "How long does it take for some coffee and a bagel? I'll make it easy. I'll meet you right here. Ray won't mind."

"You're sure he won't?" she said.

"Hey, Ray," Eddie yelled out, "is it okay if Devon and I have breakfast here next week?"

"What am I, running a restaurant here?" he yelled back.

"I'll bring you some of those lox you like," replied Eddie.

"Okay, in the office. You got twenty minutes," answered Ray.

"There," said Eddie, "we got twenty minutes."

"All that, well, how can I refuse?" Devon laughed. Eddie gave her that big smile and said this would possibly be the shortest date ever, but he'd take it, and they both agreed to meet there at seven. Eddie thanked her and went to find his men so they could get to their next job. On the way out, he stopped to hand her his business card, on which he wrote the number of his personal cellphone. He asked if she had a number where she could be reached in case he got hung up at a job and couldn't make breakfast next Monday. He handed her another of his cards, and she wrote down her cell number on the back.

"See you next week, Devon from the Catskills," he said as he took the card and left the store. Devon watched as he left and put the card in her bag and took out the list of flowers she was to pick up. She gave the list to Ray because he always filled the orders himself for Mrs. Ogden. He told her that Eddie was a prince, and she couldn't find a nicer boy; he smiled and told her they could have thirty minutes if she wanted. Devon rarely blushed, but hearing Ray mention her plans for breakfast for next week with Eddie made her face feel flushed. She chuckled to herself after Ray took the list and went to pack up the flowers. This was unexpected; definitely not in her plan, but she did say her plan was flexible, and she couldn't help but like this guy. There weren't many men in her life right now. Actually, none without JR, but she refused to let herself think about him. She had to stay busy. That was the only way she could get through the day. Nights were a different story. Devon couldn't stop her dreams.

The week went by quickly for Devon. Between the lodge and the flower shop, she ended most days completely exhausted, which was fine with her. She liked the work. A few nights she even managed to have the pool to herself. Both the lodge and the flower shop were extremely busy. The people at the lodge wanted to get in a few weeks' vacation before their children went back to school. The shop was handling a few weddings on the weekends, plus their normal work, mainly funeral pieces. The fast pace didn't bother Devon; she just ran circles around Mrs. Ogden, who couldn't help but laugh at the young dynamo. Mrs. Ogden knew the shop would be in good hands with Devon at the wheel, and she kept the secret with Devon's parents, who already came up with a price for the business and had already put one-third of the asking price down. Devon was going to be thrilled when she came home from the city after grooming school and found out that she now owned the business. Mrs. Ogden had agreed to stay on for three months to make sure Devon knew what she was doing, but she didn't have a doubt in her mind that Devon could take over tomorrow and handle it as good as she could. Devon worked at the lodge on Sunday but had an early dinner with her parents and went to bed early. Monday morning was for flower pickup and her breakfast date with Eddie. She was so excited and felt like a schoolgirl on her first date. This was so unexpected. After the last few weeks, she thought she never wanted anything to do with men.

Devon arrived at quarter to seven and saw Eddie's truck there already. She put on a little lip gloss, tousled her hair, and went into the flower shop. The brothers were hard at work filling orders, but when they saw Devon, they stopped work and came to say hello.

"Good morning, Raymond, Kevin, hope all is well," she said softly.

"All is well, business is good, we have our health, and love is in the air," spouted Raymond. "Your date awaits you in the office." Devon began to blush; this time she could really feel her face get warm.

"Look, Kevin, see how beautiful love is." He gestured toward Devon.

"Beautiful, just beautiful," said Kevin. "Go, go have breakfast." Devon searched her bag for the list of flowers she needed for the week and gave it to Raymond. Raymond put his hand to his head and commented that business must be good at the shop. This was one of the largest orders they ever filled. He even commented to his brother that with new youngblood, the business was just going to get better and better. He and his brother turned to fill the order and motioned again to Devon to enter the office. Eddie had a small, white tablecloth on top of the desk and a bud vase with a single yellow rose with some baby's breath in it.

"Good morning," she said to Eddie. "What's all this? It's wonderful. How did you know I love yellow roses?"

"I just knew you didn't look like the red rose type," replied Eddie. For a moment, Devon's head went reeling. She had heard exactly the same words before. It hurt so much, but she forced it out of her mind and took a seat. Eddie put a pile of different bagels in front of her and real cloth napkins. He poured her coffee and smiled that adorable teddy bear smile. This was such a sweet thing to do, and all the events of the last few weeks just melted away in his smile. His brown eyes sparkled like a child opening presents at Christmas, and when he smiled, there was just a small dimple in his left cheek. Devon felt so relaxed. The two of them talked all through breakfast and were so surprised when Raymond knocked on the door and told them it was a quarter to eight.

"Thank you, Raymond," said Devon as she began to pick up the remnants of breakfast. Eddie helped as best as he could, but Devon was like a small tornado, rushing this way and that.

"Slow down," he said. "Let me help."

"I'm sorry. I had no idea we talked so long, and I've got to get the flowers to the shop."

"And you will. Just slow down," replied Eddie.

"This was really fun. Thank you," said Devon, "but I wanted to tell you something before I left. I'll be starting dog grooming school next week, Monday, actually and will be living here with friends for the next few months. It will probably take me awhile to get settled, but I'll call you when I do, and we can do this again, but maybe with a little more time."

"That's great," said Eddie. "Why dog grooming school?"

"It's the next step in my plan to have my own pet shop and grooming salon as well as the flower shop, of course, and then later on, my no-kill animal sanctuary. I know it sounds impossible. Everyone thinks so, but it's a plan I've had for as long as I can remember, and I will make it happen one day," said Devon excitedly, erasing all the signs of the breakfast they just had.

"Wow, that's incredible. I can't plan tomorrow, and look at you. Just in the short time I've known you, if anyone can do it, it's going to be you." Eddie laughed. "Come on. Let's get you on the road." All the flowers were loaded in the van, and Devon quickly told the brothers that she would be going to school here in the city for a few months so would not be coming for the flowers on Monday mornings until she finished.

"What's this I'm hearing?" said Raymond. "No sunshine on Monday? Well, if you will be in the city, we can at least expect a visit from time to time, yes? A little time for some coffee and maybe a nosh. You call and I'll make sure we have that elderberry jam you like. So when do you start?"

"Next Monday," said Devon as she began to get in the van but suddenly made a mad dash back into the building to retrieve her rose.

"Can't leave this behind," she said, looking at Eddie, who had now positioned himself by the van's door.

"Don't worry. I know where I can get more." He laughed. "This has been the best and fastest forty-five-minute breakfast I've ever had," he said. "Thank you." Devon smiled and felt something pass through her. It felt good. She thoroughly surprised Eddie by kissing him gently on the lips; then she jumped into the van before he could react. Devon just pulled away smiling. As the Nardell brothers stood with Eddie on the sidewalk, Raymond was the only one who spoke.

"Such a girl you couldn't find nowhere. If this is meant to be, Eddie my boy, you will have the best life of any man." He gave Eddie a pat on the back and said they had to get back to work and that the flowers don't take care of themselves. Eddie stood for a while until he couldn't see the van anymore. He touched his lips with his fingers and said to himself that no matter what it took or how long it took, that was the girl he would marry.

Devon got back to the shop where Mrs. Ogden and the new girl she hired to help while Devon was in school were still cleaning out the coolers, changing water, and scrubbing containers. Devon immediately began to work getting the flowers clipped and put in water. The roses were put in the front cooler along with some exotics like orchids. With the way growers worked today, almost any kind of flower could be had any time of the year. Many wholesalers like the Nardell Brothers' got flowers from other countries like the Netherlands for tulips and strange-looking pods and bromeliads from South American countries. The choices were getting better and better, and Devon loved making special arrangements with these. Many of the arrangements for the lodge were made with ornamental grasses and a variety of odd-looking pods like artichoke because they lasted so long. Devon finished all the flowers, and Mrs. Ogden could not believe the selections and vibrant colors in this load, but she knew that they were almost all going to be used in the arrangements for the party being held at the lodge on Friday evening; an incredibly large engagement party for one of the local politician's daughter. Devon took the order herself and suggested some of the flowers, knowing there would be nothing like it anywhere. The couple loved her ideas and left everything up to her. Devon knew this would be her last party for a while until she finished grooming school, and she planned to make it one of her best.

The week went by so fast. The engagement party was one of the most beautiful anyone had ever seen, and Devon was sure she had created some new business for the shop. Everyone oh'd and ah'd the arrangements. The color scheme of peach and sage was perfect, and small glass bowls were in the middle of the tables, each with a colorful fish swimming in it and a corresponding colored floating candle on top. Mr. and Mrs. Taylor received so many wonderful comments on their beautiful decorating scheme that a few booked their future parties with them. They had to explain that their daughter, who was the florist, would be in school in New York City for a few months and couldn't guarantee that she could do the flower arrangements. Some suggested they would pay extra just to have her services for their parties and were sure arrangements could be made. Devon was in seventh heaven. This was the largest and most expensive party she had ever done, and she knew she nailed it, but now she had to make sure she nailed the next step in her life plan. She thought about Eddie and wondered where he would fit in. Somehow she knew he did.

On Sunday morning, the Taylors enjoyed a long breakfast together before Devon loaded her things in the car. Goodbyes were hard, but she and her dad were finally on the road to New Paltz. Rory was waiting for them with her parents, Lillian and Robert Stewart. The Stewarts assured Devon's father that they would take good care of his daughter while she was in the city with them. Warren Taylor left with so many mixed emotions. He loved Devon, and the thought of not seeing her for weeks at a time was so difficult. He had tears in his eyes, but he was also so proud of the woman she had become. Woman. Just the other day she was his little girl. How did she grow up so fast? He laughed when he remembered some of the things he shared with her as she was growing up. Theirs was a close relationship, even closer than the one she share with her mother. He vowed to do whatever was necessary to help make his daughter's dreams come true.

17

Devon's first day in class was so exciting and a little boring. Half of the day was taken up by the teacher explaining all the tools and their function, and the second half was taken up buying the books and instruments needed for the classes that were to come. Devon got everything she needed and packed them neatly in her bag. She couldn't believe that a pair of curved scissors could cost eighty dollars.

"Invest in the best equipment you can afford," the teacher said, "as they will last you a lifetime."

For eighty dollars, they damn well better, she thought. She spoke to some of the other students in the class and got a few names; all of which, she realized, she had forgotten as she left the building. *God, she thought, if I can't remember a name from three hours ago, how will I ever remember everything from class?* As she had done in the past, Devon put the past few hours neatly tucked away in a box in her head. She remembered one of her high school teachers saying that Devon could compartmentalize better than anyone. It was the only way she knew; the way she got so many things done and done well. Devon walked out of her first day of dog grooming school feeling a little letdown that the day hadn't been as exciting as she hoped. *But hopefully tomorrow would be better*, she thought. While she held the door for another student to come out of the building, she glanced up and saw Eddie leaning against his van, with a yellow rose in his hand, wearing that huge teddy bear smile.

"Yours?" said the other girl, looking at Eddie. "If not, I'll take him." Devon didn't bother to answer; she just walked up to Eddie and waited until he said something.

"This is for you," he said as he handed her the yellow rose.

"When you graduate, you get the whole dozen." Devon blushed, which was something she rarely did, but this was the second time he had made her blush.

"Thank you, kind sir," she said, not quite knowing what to say next. Devon without something to say was indeed an unusual occasion.

"So how was your first day of school?" asked Eddie.

"Frightfully boring. Half the day was spent on our teacher explaining the tools we would be using and their uses, and the other half we spent buying the tools we would be using. Can you imagine a pair of scissors that cost eighty dollars?"

"Not really. I'm guessing that they must be precision shears with a good blade that can be resharpened as needed," he replied.

"I hope you're right. I'd hate to have to replace them each time they got dull," she answered. "So to what do I owe this surprising and welcome visit?"

"I just thought a country girl like you would appreciate a smiling face after a hard day at school, especially the first day," he said.

"More likely you thought this country girl would be lost on her first day in the big city. Go ahead admit it." She laughed.

"Honestly, that never crossed my mind," he said, grinning.

"You better be careful around here. That girl that I came out of the door with was ready to pounce on your bones."

"Really?" said Eddie. "I guess you're going to have to protect me then." After a short moment of silence, Eddie asked if she had plans for dinner.

"Unfortunately I do," she said. "This is the first day with the Stewarts, and I'm sure they expect me to come straight home. I know from Rory that her mom was having some of my favorite things prepared, but any other time would be okay. I just have to tell her I won't be home for dinner. One of the rules of the house."

"Just one of the rules? Do they walk you to school too? I'm sorry. That was uncalled for. Just chalk it up to being disappointed," he replied.

"If it's any consolation, I'm disappointed too," she said, trying to make him smile again.

"Trying to make me feel better?" he answered.

"I am. How did I do?" she said.

"Good. You did good, Devon from the Catskills. Another time then. May I at least have the pleasure of your company while I take you home?"

"That's not necessary. I've been briefed on the subway system. Thank you. And besides, they live all the way up on Fifty-Ninth Street, and that must be way out of your way."

"It may well be, but at least I'll have a half hour more of your company. That's if you don't mind riding in the van," he said.

"I don't, and thank you." Eddie tried to get to the door to open it for her, but she beat him to it.

"Could you at least let me try to act like a gentleman? My mother would kill me if she saw," he said.

"Sorry. I'm just so used to doing things for myself, but I promise if your mother ever asks, I'll tell her you did. How's that?" She laughed.

"I guess it'll do. Just remember, I open all doors, walk on the outside, and wait until you are seated before I sit, and I use my napkin," he said seriously. Devon tried not to laugh but couldn't hold it in any longer. She had tears in her eyes just by the look on his face and how serious he was trying to be.

"I'm so sorry. I tried not to laugh, but you just got so serious on me. I couldn't help it," she said.

"Say you're sorry," he said.

"I'm sorry," said Devon, this time bending over with laughter.

Eddie knew he lost. *Yep*, he said to himself, *this is the one*. Devon had been right about the Stewarts making a special night for her. Dinner was wonderful. Devon's favorites: a simple meal of meatloaf, mashed potatoes with gravy, and glazed carrots. She thanked the Stewarts for dinner and asked the house rules. Mr. Stewart laughed and said that everyone was over twenty-one, and he didn't feel that they needed rules; just behave responsibly, and all would be fine. There was, however, an alarm that was usually set at around midnight on workdays, and they would give her the code and show her the operation. All they asked was that she notified the housekeeper if she would not be home for dinner. Devon said she forgot how exhausting school could be and guaranteed that she would be asleep well before midnight. She told them about Eddie and how they met and that she might see him occasionally for dinner or breakfast. Mrs. Stewart said that they should have him over for dinner some evening; perhaps the same evening Rory could invite her young man. And there would be six for dinner; a wonderful number for conversation.

Devon told her that she loved the idea of dinner but would like to hold off until she really got into a routine. Devon explained how she needed to be in a routine for a while before adding something new, and Mr. Stewart agreed with her wholeheartedly and said it was a very sensible approach to new circumstances. With dinner out of the way and coffee served, conversation was mostly about Rory, which was fine with Devon; then the Stewarts retired, and she and Rory had time to catch up on things, especially the guys they were dating. And Rory said they must double date sometime. Devon looked at the time and told Rory that she would like to call home. Rory said good night, and Devon called the lodge, knowing her parents would be waiting for her call. She told them about her day and how she missed them already; she told them she loved them and said good night. Devon was asleep as soon as her head hit the pillow.

The weeks flew by as Devon tried desperately to remember everything taught in class, but loving what she was doing made it seem like child's play. The Stewarts had Eddie over for dinner, which went very well. Eddie and Rory's boyfriend, Mark, got along great; both were sports nuts. They planned a trip for the four of them to go to a hockey game at Madison Square Garden. Rory and Mark were both third year students at Fordham studying law. Rory planned on entering her parents' law firm of corporate law, but Mark was still undecided about what field he was going into, which created some interesting conversation at dinner; even Eddie got into the conversation explaining the problems with his business from accidents or complaints. Devon watched the five of them all trying to talk at once and thought it somehow felt just like home. Rory, Mark, she, and Eddie got together regularly for dinner or sports event and had such fun. Eddie complained at first, saying he wouldn't fit in, but he was so wrong; everyone loved him, especially Mark, and soon the two of them became best friends. Devon couldn't believe she only had a few months to go, and she would have to go back to the Catskills; she would miss this.

Devon learned quickly about the subway system and the people who rode them. Most were just eager to go to work in the morning and go home at night, but on occasion, there were a few that liked to harass people and bother pretty young girls. Mark gave Devon a few suggestions on how to avoid any trouble with them, but one evening, she found herself right in the middle of a serious situation. She had gotten out of class late, walked to the subway, and got on the train that would take her uptown. She was sitting down, trying to read a magazine on different dog breeds, making no eye contact with anyone, but remaining very alert about things going on around her when two African American men walked into the car through the doors from another car. They were asking everyone for money, but no one gave them any, which seemed to be making them angry. They approached Devon. The older one sat down next to her and asked for some money. She said she had none to give. Then he started to tell his friend how such a beautiful thing like that didn't have any money. His friend laughed and said she probably did because she looked like one of those rich girls from uptown.

"Is that right, pretty? You one of them rich uptown girls?" said the man sitting next to her. Devon just tried to ignore him.

"Pretty, I said is that right?" But Devon continued to ignore him.

"Didn't yo mama tell you it ain't polite to ignore someone talking to you?" he said. Devon asked him to please leave her alone.

"Look at that. She says please. Your mama taught you well. Then why you ignoring me, pretty?" he said as he drew even closer so that Devon couldn't hold her magazine. She jumped off the seat, grabbed the center pole and put her magazine in her bag. As she pushed the book into her bag, she felt her curved scissors lying on the bottom. The two men followed her, with the older one standing behind her, touching her hair.

"Mmm, you sure does smell good," he said. "Why don't you and me go over in the corner and gets to know one another better, pretty?" Devon tried to move away from him, but the other man pushed her from the other side, closer to the one who was doing all the talking. She could smell them; a combination of urine and body odor and definitely liquor of some kind. They both had rotten teeth, and she could smell the decay. She doubted if they ever brushed their teeth. Devon was not usually prone to panic, but something told her she was in trouble. She watched carefully out the window as the stations went by. If she could just make it to Thirty-Fourth Street, she would quickly get off and start running until she was in a crowd of people or better yet saw a cop. Her mind was in panic mode, and she knew she needed to get in control if she was going to get out of this mess. The older man came up closer behind her and started to rub against her. She could feel him grinding into her, speaking to her as he did.

"Now don't that feels real good, pretty? I knows you like it now, don't ya? Don't be shy. We all good here," he said. The man on the other side of Devon just laughed and told his friend that she liked it. "Do some more," he said. The older man grabbed Devon by the chin and spun her around facing him and tried to kiss her, but Devon pulled away, which angered the man, and he hit her with the back of his hand. Devon could feel her lip bleeding. She looked around the subway car, hoping someone would help her, but no one seemed to notice. They were all too afraid for themselves. Devon had enough. She knew she should probably stay quiet, but she couldn't. She turned, looked at him directly in his eyes, and said if he touched her again, he'd be sorry.

"Look here, Junior. This one's got a little fire in her. I likes fire," he said and backhanded Devon again. This time, Devon felt her nose take the hit from that strike and felt her warm blood start to run down into her mouth.

"Now, looks at what you made me do, pretty. I ain'ts a mean man. Just you ask Junior here, but no woman sasses me. Hear me, pretty? Now lets me hear how sorry you is. Come on, say it." And he grabbed a handful of Devon's hair and pulled until her head was yanked back. The man on the other side of her was so occupied watching his friend; he didn't notice Devon slip her hand into her bag. She felt around the bottom of the bag, trying to move slowly. She found the scissors and grabbed them tightly in her hand. She knew that the subway would be stopping at Thirty-Fourth Street any minute. The train soon stopped and opened the doors. Devon waited just a few seconds then pulled out the scissors and stabbed the man behind her in the thigh then pushed her way past the other man and ran for the stairs as fast as she could. She kept running until she got to the next level and spotted two policemen. She ran straight into them and pleaded for them to help her. She told them her story, and one police officer radioed in the attack while the other took her to a place where she could sit down and tried to stop the blood running from her nose. They also radioed for a med unit. Devon kept insisting she was all right, but the police officer told her it was standard practice to have them look at her. Just as she was trying to stop the bleeding from her nose, she spotted a couple walking by them.

"Stop them. Right there. They were on the subway. They saw what happened!" she yelled. The police stopped the elderly couple and asked them what they saw. At first they said they didn't see anything, but Devon got up and went to them and asked them to please tell the officers what they saw. After they saw Devon's face, the woman explained what they saw but said that they would not go to court to testify; they were too frightened. They had to ride the subway every day, and it could be one of them next time. Devon thanked them then sat back down; her head reeling from the blows she took to her face.

They took the names of the couple and let them go. Devon asked if she could make a call. She knew the Stewarts wouldn't be home, it being the Wednesday before Thanksgiving. They went to Colorado or someplace for the holiday and to ski. She knew she couldn't call home. She didn't want to upset her parents; and by the time they got to New York, it would all be over. The only one left was Eddie. She prayed she could reach him, and she did. Eddie said he would be there as fast as he could and if they took her to a hospital to call him again. The emergency team arrived in no time, checked her vitals, asked about any health conditions, and placed a cold bag behind her neck while she pinched the top of her nose. It wasn't Devon's first bloody nose. Her lip was swelling rapidly, and her head began to ache; suddenly she began to shake.

One of the medics put a blanket around her and told her she was safe. He guessed that she was having a little post-traumatic shock. After checking her vitals again and saw how her lip and nose were swelling, they decided to take her to the hospital. Devon claimed that she was fine, but the medic said that she might need a CAT scan, and her nose might be broken. She quickly called Eddie when they told her which hospital they were taking her. Devon closed her eyes in the ambulance, remembering what just happened to her, and began to shake again. The medic who was with her in the back of the ambulance kept assuring her that she was safe and there was nothing to worry about. After being examined by the ER doctor, he told her that her nose was not broken and the CAT scan was clear. The doctor who had her case told her that she was extremely lucky; funny, she didn't feel lucky. Eddie arrived just as two policemen were in her room taking her statement. They asked to see the scissors that she said she stabbed one of them with. Devon told them they were in her bag. One of the policemen emptied the contents of the bag on the table and, with a gloved hand, put them into a plastic evidence bag, sealed it, and wrote something on it. He told her that they had to take them to the forensics lab. Devon insisted she needed them for school, but he promised that she would get them back when they were done. A call came in on one of their radios saying that the two men were apprehended at the next stop, and they were taking the one Devon stabbed to the hospital. Devon felt a small relief that the two were caught.

"What happens now?" asked Devon.

"Once you're released from the hospital, we'll need you to come down to the station to make a formal statement, and you may have to view them in a lineup. After that, you can go. We will check on the background of the two assailants, and most likely, they have some kind of record. If we're lucky, they may be on probation, and that means back to jail for them. Either way, you won't have to worry. They will be behind bars," said one of the officers. The doctor came in and told her everything looked fine but that he wanted her to go straight home and gave her a prescription for some painkillers.

"But I have to go down to the police station," she said. The doctor asked if it couldn't wait until tomorrow, that she was in significant pain, and he didn't want her running around because of the blows she took to the face. The officers deferred to the doctor and said she could come down tomorrow, took her scissors, and left. After the police left, Eddie rushed to her bedside, looking more frightened than her. The doctor looked at Eddie and asked if he was there for her. Eddie shook his head, and the doctor said that he wanted her to go straight home, keep the ice on her face, and come back to the hospital immediately if she felt nauseated or her headache was getting worse. Devon signed her discharge papers and took the prescription. She looked at Eddie standing there worried, and she tried to assure him that she was okay. She explained that she didn't know who to call since the Stewarts were out of town and her parents so far away. Eddie took her hand and told her she did the right thing and that he would have been angry if she hadn't called him. He helped her off the bed, and a nurse came with a wheelchair, which Devon refused. The nurse explained it was hospital policy and she had to use it. Devon sighed and sat in the chair. She was fine and hated all the fuss they were making over her.

Eddie ran out to get the van and pulled it up to the doors and got out to help Devon. She wanted to scream that she was fine and could do it herself, but she didn't. She was so glad he was here with her. Eddie pulled away from the hospital and headed downtown. Devon didn't even ask where they were going, just tried to keep the ice bag on her face, which hurt like hell. In a short time, Eddie pulled the van into a warehouse somewhere near the Little Italy section of the city. He helped Devon out of the van and told her that he needed to lock up the warehouse and set the alarm and that his place was next door. Devon counted at least five vans in the warehouse before they left.

Eddie set the alarms and opened the door to his apartment for her. She was surprised when she entered the apartment. It was really quite nice; a bit masculine, but after all, a man did live there. Not fully furnished but not Spartan either; a nice blend of furnishings. Some looked antique, some oriental. She really wasn't in the mood to discuss his taste in decor as her head felt like it was bursting, but she would like to know who decorated the apartment.

Eddie showed her into a bedroom and told her to make herself comfortable. He asked if she felt well enough for him to leave for a while to get her script filled and that if he hurried, he could get there before they closed. She said she was fine and lay down on the bed. Eddie promised he would be back as soon as he could, and he'd get more ice bags. Devon heard him lock the door, and she closed her eyes. She must have fallen asleep but awoke when she heard the door open. She felt so defenseless and scared. What if it wasn't Eddie? What would she do? She crept up to the back of the bed and folded her legs under, trying to make herself look as small as possible. She gripped the blanket and held it close and began to shake.

"Hey, hey, what's the matter? It's only me," said Eddie as he saw the terrified look on her face. "I'm sorry. I guess I should have called out to let you know it was me. I didn't mean to frighten you."

"No, it's just me. I guess I'm a little more shaken up than I thought," she answered.

"I got your pills and some more of those ice bags. What would you like to take your pills with?" he asked. Then he asked if she had anything to eat tonight. She told him she hadn't eaten anything since breakfast and didn't think she could anyway. But he insisted she had to eat something with these painkillers and was making her some toast and some tea. Before he left, he went to the dresser and got out a clean pajama top and gave it to her. He told her the bathroom was to the left, and he would get her some fresh towels if she wanted to shower. She wasn't sure she felt well enough to stand and shower, but she definitely needed to wash off the smell of that man. She made her way to the bathroom and looked in the mirror at her swollen face; the right side was already turning black and blue. Her lip was also split on the outer edge. She stood against the sink and started to shake, but this time, she managed to talk herself out of it; she soon got in control. She refused to let some creep get the best of her and climbed into the shower. The water felt good, cleaning away all the horror of the last few hours. Eddie must have put the towels out while she was in the shower. She wrapped herself in a large one, and it felt warm. It felt so good, so relaxing. She finished up in the bathroom and returned to the bedroom where Eddie was waiting with her tea, toast, and a glass of water. It was strange that she didn't even feel self-conscious, clad only in his pajama top, but since it almost reached her knees, there wasn't any reason to feel self-conscious; it was like wearing a dress. He laughed when he saw her and commented that now she was wearing the latest in fashion. She tried to laugh, but her lip hurt too much. She climbed into bed, had some tea and toast, took her pill, and was about to thank him; but he pulled up the covers and told her to get some rest and that he would be right outside on the couch if she needed anything. She was too exhausted to fight with him, so she snuggled down, pulling the covers up around herself. Eddie told her that he would be in with another ice bag in an hour, closed the door partway, and left.

Devon could feel herself drifting off to sleep when suddenly she was back in the subway; the smell filling her nose, that voice in her ear, his body pushing against her, and she screamed. Eddie raced to her in seconds, taking her up in his arms, holding her tightly, telling her that it was all right, and that she was safe. She heard his voice but still couldn't get the drama of the last few hours out of her head. He stroked her hair and kept telling her that she was safe, and that he would never let anything happen to her. She knew he was trying to make her feel better, but she also knew there was no way he could really keep her safe; tonight proved it.

Devon awoke to the smell of coffee and followed the scent. Eddie was in the kitchen preparing a tray.

"Coffee smells great," she said.

"Hey, what are you doing out of bed? I was just bringing it in to you," he replied.

"I'm fine. Thank you, but I don't need to be treated like a china doll," said Devon.

"Boy, you really are independent, aren't you?" answered Eddie. "Okay then, fix your own coffee. What would you like toast or toast?" he asked.

"Just coffee," she answered.

"No, not just coffee. White or whole wheat?" he answered back. By the look on his face, she knew she was going to have toast if she wanted it or not. She laughed to herself, watching this big bear of a man so at home in the kitchen. She wondered if he grew up the way she had, with all the family welcomed in the kitchen preparing meals together.

"How old are you?" she asked.

"Why, how old do I look?" he replied.

"No, I just meant you look very comfortable around a kitchen. I wondered how long you've been on your own."

"In our house, if you wanted to eat, you learned really quickly how to put two slices of bread together with something inside. I have three sisters and a brother, and I am the middle child. My two older sisters took care of themselves, and my mother was always looking after the two younger ones, so that left me to fend for myself. I'm twenty-six and have had my own place for about four years," he said. "Anything else you'd like to know?"

"Much more but I'll leave it for another time. Do you remember what time the cops said to be at the station, and today's Thanksgiving, don't they get days off?" Devon heard herself say it was Thanksgiving and something registered in her head that she wouldn't be spending it with her parents. She put down her coffee, closed her eyes, and sighed.

"What's wrong?" he asked.

"I was looking forward to spending today with my parents. I haven't been home in three weeks, and now it looks like I'll miss the holiday too," she said sadly. Nothing but silence, then suddenly Eddie spoke up and said that she wouldn't miss the holiday with her parents.

"Finish your coffee. Go get dressed, and we will get to the station to give them your statement. While you're getting dressed, I'll call my mom, explain things, and then we'll go to the Catskills," he said all in one breath.

"No, you've done enough already. I won't let you miss the holiday with your family. Just drop me off at the Stewarts if you would. I'll be fine," said Devon.

"Not a chance. I've always wanted to see the Catskills, and I hear it's beautiful this time of year," he answered.

"No, Eddie, it's not right. You should be with family today!" she yelled back.

"And I will be. Just not mine. Now get dressed." That was a clear, definite order, and Devon wasn't sure how she felt about it, but she got up and went to dress. She hated to put on the same clothes, but since she had nothing else, she had to. She really just wanted to throw them in the trash and burn them. The thought of them against her skin made her skin crawl, but she put them on and said nothing.

When she came out of the bedroom, Eddie went in and returned a few minutes with an overnight and garment bag. Devon hadn't even thought about him having to stay over. He relayed warm wishes from his mom that she should feel better soon and to enjoy her holiday with her parents.

"That's all she said?"

"No, she said to tell you not to let me eat too much," and he laughed. He unplugged the coffeepot and rinsed it out, took out the grinds, and placed them in the freezer. He noticed Devon looking at him as if he was crazy and said he would come back to a smelly place if he didn't do that. He was always a surprise.

The trip to the police station took no time at all. She gave her statement and picked their picture out of a book and was told that she needn't worry about those two, that they were both on probation, and their attack on her put them automatically back in prison, plus the fact that one of them was carrying a weapon, a twenty-two; small, but just as deadly as any other gun. Shivers went down Devon's spine when she thought of the possibility that she might have been shot. She also got her scissors back, which was a major relief. In less than an hour, they were on their way to the lodge and home. Devon gave Eddie directions for the easiest route and made him promise to say nothing about the gun in front of her parents. From the look of her face, they would have to be told what happened, but they didn't need to know it could have been worse. Eddie promised.

18

THEY ARRIVED AT THE lodge, stopping once to get breakfast; half a piece of toast and a cup of coffee was all Devon had, and he was determined that she had a proper breakfast. She argued with him again and lost again. Devon finished everything and realized that she really was hungry, and the breakfast hit the spot. As they got back in the van, Eddie kidded her about how much she ate. She told him she was afraid he would have force-fed her if she didn't eat it all. He laughed and said she was finally learning that he would take care of her when he saw that she wasn't. Their conversation during the ride covered topics from family to jokes and everything in between. It was such an enjoyable ride that Devon silently wished it was just a little longer; however, it was so good to be home.

"Welcome to the lodge and my home," said Devon.

"Wow, this is impressive," replied Eddie. "It's larger than the warehouse and then some. Just beautiful. Really, really beautiful." The lodge showed very well in the fall. The log walls gleamed golden as if they had been polished, and the large windows had a clear view of the pond on the other side. Most of the deciduous trees had dropped their foliage, but some clung to their leaves as if they were too beautiful to give up—the reds, oranges, and yellows. The pine and spruce trees were an excellent background for the hanging leaves. All the fall mums in shades to match the leaves were blooming in the gardens around the porch, which was filled with rocking chairs. Even the second story had flower boxes outside the windows filled with bunches of the colored mums and leaves. Eddie said that this was the finest place he had ever seen and should have come to the Catskills earlier but then corrected himself and said that it probably wouldn't look this good if he hadn't been here with her. Devon took his hand and led him into her home. She peered through the window and saw both her mother and father at the front desk.

"Eddie, I need your help. My parents are both at the front desk, and I don't want to talk to them right now. I want to run to my room, get these clothes off, and jump in the shower quickly. Do you think you can kill some time until I get back down?"

"I guess for you I could be creative, but don't take too long," he replied. She reached up, kissed him, told him he was the best, and led him up the stairs and through the door. Her parents both looked toward the door as it opened and were totally surprised to see their daughter. She usually took the train, and they picked her up in Hudson. Devon hurried to them, hugged and kissed each of them, introduced them to Eddie, and was off before her parents could even say hello or get a good look at her face. They looked at each other, then at Eddie, who was standing there, trying to think of something to say and decided to wait until they spoke first but then changed his mind.

Best defense is a good offense, he thought.

"Mr. and Mrs. Taylor, I have to say Devon really didn't tell me how beautiful your place is," said Eddie.

"Thank you, Eddie," said Mrs. Taylor. "Can I get you anything while we wait for Devon to come back? I'm sorry, but can you tell me where in the world she ran off to and why?" Eddie wasn't sure exactly what to say but thought honesty was the best way to go, especially seeing the look on Mr. Taylor's face.

"I would love some coffee, if it isn't too much trouble," he said, "and Devon needed to get out of her clothes and take a quick shower." Now he did it; both of her parents took a step closer toward him.

"Look, I don't mean to sound cryptic, but it's a long story, and I think Devon would really prefer to explain it herself." Devon's mom didn't have a reply for Eddie; she just walked to a large urn by the wall, picked up a mug, filled it with coffee, and asked Eddie if he would like sugar and cream. Eddie replied that black was just fine. She returned and handed him the mug. Eddie sipped the coffee, hoping they would hold all questions until Devon got back.

"How long have you known our daughter?" asked her father.

"Since the middle of August. I met her one morning when she was picking up flowers in New York," replied Eddie.

"Oh, so you work in the flower business," said Devon's mother.

"No, I have my own business and was there to get the walk-in coolers up and running. They shorted out around four in the morning, and my crew and I were there to fix the problem," he replied.

"And where was this?" she asked.

"The Nardell's. You know Raymond and Kevin. I was told by Devon that they got most of their flowers from them. She came in to get the flowers, and Raymond introduced me to her. We spoke for a while as my crew was cleaning up. I even asked her out, but she told me how she lived up here. Pretty far for a date. So I asked her to have breakfast with me the next time she made a trip down to the city."

"And did you have breakfast with our daughter?" said Mrs. Taylor softly. Eddie looked at Mr. Taylor as he stood, gripping the edge of the counter and thought he might as well continue.

"Funny you should ask. As a matter of fact, we did. Raymond let us use his office while his men were loading her van with the flowers. I bought a few bagels and some coffee, and we had breakfast," answered Eddie.

"What he's leaving out is the way he had it set up," said Devon, having just returned, with her hair still damp. "He had a white tablecloth over the desk, a bud vase with a yellow rose, all different kinds of bagels, and cream cheese, even lox."

"I didn't really know what she liked," said Eddie, "so I had to get a little of everything." Mrs. Taylor smiled at him, then turned to her daughter and saw her face fully for the first time.

"My god, Devon, your face!" she screamed.

"Mom, keep it down please. The whole place can hear you. Could we please go into the office, and I'll tell you everything. Just let me grab a cup of coffee." While Devon got her coffee, Mr. Taylor asked one of the girls to mind the desk, and that they were going to the office. They both led the way while Eddie waited for Devon.

"Thank you," she said as she walked to the office with Eddie following close behind. She approached the office door, which was closed, and turned around and kissed Eddie. He just smiled that adorable ear-to-ear smile that showed the small dimple in his cheek. Devon knew in that instant that she was falling in love. She opened the door and said to him, "Here goes nothing."

"I know you both have a lot of questions, but let me explain what happened first. Then if you still have questions, I'll try to answer them," she said. Devon explained in as much detail as she could remember the events of the last two days. When she had finished, she turned to Eddie and asked him if she left anything out. Eddie said no and that she covered it all. The Taylors were horrified by their daughter's story. Devon's mother hugged her daughter then looked more closely at her face.

"Oh, you poor thing. Your lip, it looks so sore," she said.

"Does it hurt much?"

Devon smiled. "Not as much as yesterday, Mom."

Devon's father rose from his seat and stood in front of Eddie. He put out his hand, and Eddie took it. "I don't know how we can thank you for rescuing our daughter."

"I'm just glad I was there to help, Mr. Taylor," said Eddie. Devon's father gently slapped Eddie on the back. You could tell that he was so choked up. He just didn't know what to say. Finally, Devon stepped up to her father, and they hugged one another. He just realized that he could have lost her and began to tear up. Devon felt his tears wet on her face and told him over and over that she was fine. He finally let go of her and reached for a handkerchief in his pocket. Devon looked at Eddie, and he had tears in his eyes too. She reached up and gently wiped them away.

"Let's see that big smile," she said. Eddie couldn't help but start laughing and smiling, and as he did, so did all of them. Devon's mother and father held her close for a few seconds more, then Devon broke away and said, "What does a person have to do to get some food around here?" The somber mood was broken, and everyone was laughing again. They left the office and walked to a table by a large window overlooking the pond and told Eddie to sit and asked him what he would like to eat. He said anything was fine with him, but Devon told her parents that they would like some of the chef's incredible minestrone soup, and they would split a Reuben. Devon's dad sat down with them and told his wife what he would like, and she ran off to the kitchen to order their meals.

"So you've never been to the Catskills before, Eddie?" asked Devon's father.

"No, sir, this is my first time, and I can see that I've really been missing something. It's just as Devon described, only better," he answered.

"Wait till you see it in the winter when everything is covered with a foot of snow. It's like a magical place," said Devon's father. "There is something wonderful in every season, but the winters turn the place into something out of a book. Am I right, Devon?"

"Your right, Dad. I always imagined that Santa Claus must have a place like this, and if he didn't, he should." Devon's father told Eddie what the place was like before when his grandfather owned it and the changes his dad made and finally, all remodeling and improvements that he did. When he spoke about the air-conditioning and heating systems that he just had installed this past summer, Eddie's eyes flashed. Finally something he knew to talk about. He told Mr. Taylor about the company he owned, and Mr. Taylor asked him to take a look at the system he just put in after lunch. Eddie said he would be glad to. Devon just rolled her eyes, got up, and said she was going to help her mother.

"I guess Devon has heard enough shoptalk," said her dad.

"I guess so, sir, or it was just her subtle way of letting us get to know one another a little," said Eddie.

"Subtle? Not Devon." Her father laughed. Eddie agreed with him that sometimes she was more like a steamroller. Eddie said if it weren't for her lack of subtlety but extreme quick thinking, she might never have gotten out of a bad situation. Devon's father agreed. He said he had mixed feelings about her going to the city for those classes, but he knew if there was anything to handle, she would, and he was so proud of her. Eddie said he should tell her. It would mean a lot coming from him because Devon often told him how wonderfully close they were but would like to hear that they were proud of her and recognized that she was a grown woman who could take care of herself.

"Thank you, Eddie. I will and thank you again for taking such good care of her," said Mr. Taylor.

"It's my pleasure, sir," answered Eddie.

"Do I detect some feelings for my daughter?" said Mr. Taylor.

"Yes, sir, you do," answered Eddie, "and she does for me. She just doesn't know it yet." Devon's dad slapped him on the back again.

"By the stars, I like you, son," replied Devon's father, laughing.

"Who likes who?" said Devon as she returned with her mother and their lunch.

"I like this man right here, Devon, this man right here," as he slapped Eddie's back again, making Eddie's face begin to turn red.

With lunch finished, Eddie and Devon's father took off to check out the new heating and cooling systems, which gave Devon and her mom a few minutes to talk.

"Before we clean up, is there anything you want to tell me?" asked her mom.

"About what?" replied Devon.

"About anything you haven't already," answered her mom.

"No, not really. I told you everything about the incident on the subway. Honestly, I have, and school is going great. Living with the Stewarts is wonderful. Do you know they have a housekeeper that is a Cordon Bleu-trained chef? Her dinners are to die for," said Devon.

"Okay, how about Eddie? Anything you care to tell me about him?" Devon was silent for a moment, then turned to her mom and smiled.

"After JR, I just threw myself into my work harder than ever, convinced I'd never care for anyone like that again, but call it fate or kismet or whatever. I meet this guy, and suddenly there's joy back in my life," said Devon. "I don't know what I can tell you about Eddie. It's something you have to see for yourself, and I think Dad already has. He's intelligent, considerate, responsible, funny, loves family and friends. He's always the first to reach out his hand to a stranger. He does get angry, but in a minute, it's gone. We've double dated with Rory and Mark, and they adore him, especially Mark. They even went together themselves to some sports thing at the Garden. Rory and I went once with them, and they decided the next time to leave us home, and they did. Both Rory and Mark are going to Fordham, and Eddie may look like he doesn't belong with that set because of his business, but he seems to fit in anywhere. He's incredible."

"Well, I guess I will have to see for myself," replied her mother. "Anyone who could put that sparkle back in your eyes must be special indeed. Now how about we get these things into the kitchen, and maybe you should take a short nap. We are having dinner at seven thirty, so there's plenty of time," said her mother.

"I think I will," said Devon. They cleaned up the table, and Devon went to her room to lie down. Mrs. Taylor checked on things in the kitchen and on the guests they had staying with them for the holiday weekend, hoping it would snow, and maybe they could get in a little skiing. The forecast did call for snow, but nothing was happening yet.

Devon's father and Eddie returned from the cellar, and Mr. Taylor didn't look very happy.

"Everything all right, Warren?" she asked.

"Not if Eddie's right about things, it's not," he replied gruffly.

"Well, let's not spoil the holiday. There's nothing to be done now anyway," she said, trying to lighten his mood.

"Eddie, you did plan to stay for the weekend, didn't you?"

"If you have room for me, I'd love to stay," he replied.

"Of course, we have room for you. For what you did for our daughter, we will always have room for you. Did you bring clothes with you?" she asked.

"I did. They're in the van. Where would you like me to park the van, by the way. I don't think you want it sitting at your front door," he replied.

"Let me give you a hand, Eddie," said Mr. Taylor. "I'll show you where to park. If we get snow during the night, we need to get the plow out."

Thanksgiving dinner was incredible. It was everything you could possibly want, from appetizer to elaborate desserts. Everyone who stayed at the lodge for the holiday was still talking about the dinner hours later. Around eleven o'clock, it began to snow, and the skiers all cheered and gave a toast for a good snowfall. Devon and Eddie stayed in the lounge, listening to music for a while, when Devon grabbed Eddie's hand and told him to follow her. She led him up the stairway then turned left and through a door. The hallway led toward the family's bedrooms. They passed the bedrooms and went through another door and entered a small room.

One wall of the room had a huge picture window, and there was an enormous skylight. In front of the window on the floor was a lounging couch similar to those found downstairs in front of the huge fireplaces; it was nicely padded with backs on them, just right to warm up after a day of skiing. Devon sat down and motioned for Eddie to sit next to her. She told him to reach behind and let the back down as she was doing on her side. With the back lying flat on the floor, Devon lay back, and Eddie followed. Devon told Eddie not to say anything but watch the snow falling down. After a few minutes, Devon broke the silence.

"Isn't it wonderful? I used to lie here for hours and watch the snow falling just like it is now. A few years back, when dad was remodeling this end of the lodge, he built this little room for me. I would always do my homework here because it was so peaceful. As the seasons began to change, I would come here to see if I could watch it. Pretty silly when you think about it," said Devon.

"No, not silly at all," replied Eddie. "It's like a fairy tale place. Somewhere you can watch not just the trees or snow but the elves and fairies that live here."

"Are you making fun of me?"

"Definitely not," said Eddie. "I love this place. I bet you get to see deer from up here."

"Yeah, sometimes there are so many I can't count them all. I think I've seen just about every wild thing we have around here." Eddie placed his hands behind his head.

"I could really get used to this," he said.

"Could you really?" asked Devon. "Would you miss living in the city?"

"Having lived there all my life, I really don't know, but this is like another world. Maybe I'd get bored here, but I don't think so.

Why, is it important?" he asked. Devon turned over toward Eddie and kissed him and snuggled up close to him. Eddie put his arms around her.

"I'd just want you to be happy, that's all," said Devon. Eddie pulled her closer and told her that wherever she was, he would be happy.

The next morning at breakfast, Mr. Taylor asked Eddie if he liked to ride along with him as he plowed the surrounding area around the lodge. Eddie was excited to go. He had never been on a snowplow before. The night brought about eight inches of snow, and it was still lightly falling, plus there was a bit of freezing rain, just enough to make walking difficult; and all Eddie had were his shoes with the leather soles, so he was slipping and sliding all the way to the garage. He almost fell once, making Mr. Taylor laugh.

"Don't break anything," he said. "Devon will kill me."

"I'm fine, sir, but next time I'll remember to bring winter gear," replied Eddie.

"The weather can change here on the mountain, good or bad, in no time at all," said Mr. Taylor.

They reached the garage and climbed into the truck with a plow affixed to the front. It was a pretty good-sized truck and plow, and Mr. Taylor told Eddie that he had seen it snow up to four feet overnight. Great for the skiers, but not so good for traveling the roads. The county was diligent about plowing, but private roads, such as where the lodge was on, needed to be plowed by them. He told Eddie he used to have a man come and plow, but some seasons, it cost him a fortune, so they decided to buy the truck and plow and do it themselves. They plowed the parking lot and had asked the guests who had cars to please move them to the other side while he plowed the side by the front of the lodge. Mr. Taylor commented that it was a little slick out there as he continued plowing down the road near the pond. Whether the rain was heavier near the pond and froze earlier, Mr. Taylor was having a hard time keeping the huge truck from sliding. As he rounded the last corner to head back to the lodge, he lost control, and the truck began to slide sideways. Try as he could, he couldn't get control, and the truck slid sideways off the road and overturned. Several people who were outside saw the truck turn over and immediately ran into the lodge to get help. Devon told her mom to call 911 and tell them the truck overturned and that they didn't know if anyone was injured but to send the EMTs just in case. Devon grabbed her boots and coat and ran to the truck, falling several times on the now sleet-covered road. She reached the truck and climbed up to check her father and Eddie; both men looked unconscious. Devon called their names over and over. Neither man had their seat belts on, so they were thrown around inside the truck with her father lying against Eddie. There was nothing Devon could do but wait with some of the lodge guests for emergency help. The wait seemed like an eternity, especially since the temperature had dropped at an alarming rate. Devon had forgotten her hat or gloves, and the freezing drizzle made standing in one spot for long unbearable. Everyone cheered as the emergency vehicle and a police car arrived. Since Devon knew most of the sheriff's deputies, she quickly told them what happened and who were in the truck. They tried to open the door on the truck, and one of the EMTs got in to see how the men were. Both of them were now conscious, and Mr. Taylor tried to move off Eddie but screamed out with pain. Another sheriff's car arrived and tried to give the EMTs a hand getting Mr. Taylor out on a backboard. Eddie's head was bleeding, but he managed with some assistance to pull himself out of the truck. Vitals were taken on both men and called in. Mr. Taylor was loaded into the ambulance on the gurney, and Eddie sat against the seat. He didn't look good. They decided not to wait for a second ambulance for Eddie and took off with them both. Fortunately, Catskill had a small hospital, and they were taken there to determine the extent of their injuries. Devon walked up the hill back to the lodge to inform her mother that they were both conscious and were on their way to the hospital. Devon's mother insisted that she had to go to the hospital. Devon knew better than to try to talk her out of it. One of the girls was asked to take over the desk, and the handyman was asked to wait with the truck, and that a tow truck was going to try and get it up out of the ditch as soon as the sanding truck that the deputy called for arrived. Just as Devon and her mom were pulling out of the driveway, JR pulled in with his truck. He jumped out and ran to their car as Devon was getting out of hers. She ran into his arms. The smell of him, the special soap he used imported from England for his dry skin, the smell of the apples; for a sliver of a second, she was transported back to a time in August when the only thing on their minds was to make love. She pulled away quickly as the present caught up with her, and she remembered he was her brother.

"I heard about the accident on my scanner. Who was in the truck? Where's your father?" he asked.

"Father and Eddie were plowing, and the truck turned over. They took them to the hospital. That's where we were going," answered Devon.

"Not in this vehicle, you're not. The roads are a sheet of ice. Park your car, and I'll take you," said JR. Devon did as she was told, and she and her mother got into his truck. JR had not exaggerated. The roads were all ice, and their SUV would never have made it up the hill to the hospital. JR had difficulty, but eventually, they made it to the hospital.

She and her mother ran to the desk and explained who they were and that they needed information about Warren Taylor and Eddie Griffin who were just brought in by ambulance. They were told that Mr. Taylor was in surgery and that Mr. Griffin was just transported by helicopter to Albany Medical Center. When Devon asked about their condition and injuries, she was told that she could not give them any information about that. They would have to speak to the doctor. Devon asked where they should wait so they could speak to the doctor after the surgery on her father, and the nurse directed them to a small waiting room. Devon took her mother there to sit down because she was as white as a sheet. Devon's mother was strong for everyone, but when it came to Devon's father, Carolyn fell apart. Devon asked JR if he could get her mother a cup of coffee; sugar, no cream. JR returned with the coffee just as a woman was handing Devon two small plastic bags. One contained the personal effects for her father, and the other was Eddie's. Devon gave the coffee to her mother and made her take a sip. Carolyn did but then just put the coffee on the table. Devon picked up the bag that said W. Taylor on it and gave it to her mother, who took it and held it to her chest. Devon sat next to her mother, trying to comfort her but with little effect.

"I have to find out about Eddie," she said to JR and returned to the front desk.

"Hi, I know you told me that Eddie Griffin was transported to Albany Med, but can't you give me any information about his condition?" she pleaded. The woman at the desk said she was sorry that unless she was a family member, she couldn't give out that information. Devon told her that his family was in the city, and he was here with her for the holiday. The woman asked if they were engaged, and Devon immediately said yes; they just got engaged. The woman shuffled through some papers and told her that Mr. Griffin had a severe concussion and that there was brain swelling and so was transported to the head trauma unit at Albany. Devon stepped back until she could feel the wall. She needed it to help her remain grounded. She felt light-headed and nauseated. JR asked if she was all right, but it sounded as if his voice was far, far away. When she didn't answer, he took her by the shoulders and turned her around to face him.

"Devon," said JR. "Get yourself together. Your mother needs you, and what the hell happened to your face?" Devon looked up at him and fell against him.

"I'm fine, JR, just needed a momentary shut down. Right now I wish I had five more of me. One for my mother, one for Eddie, one for the lodge, one for the flower shop, and one for school."

"What about you?" he said.

"I plan to crawl into bed, pull the covers over my head, and stay there until I wake up from this nightmare," she replied.

"No, Devon, you're stronger than this. The old Ledger line is 'You got to do what you got to do.' You may as well learn it," said JR. "Sometimes it's all you got."

"Right," replied Devon, who felt like she had just aged a hundred years. "I'll check on Mom, and then I have to call Eddie's parents." Her mother was sitting in the exact position as before, still clutching the plastic bag. The other bag was lying in a chair away from them, so JR picked it up to place it closer to Devon's mother so someone didn't walk off with it. As he went to put it down, he saw the small, blue velvet box.

"I guess you weren't kidding about being engaged," he said to Devon. She looked at him strangely then noticed the blue box he was pointing to. Devon looked at it through the plastic, then she opened the bag, removed the box, and opened it. Inside was a gold ring. An Irish claddagh, a ring of two hands holding a heart and a crown. The hands denote friendship, the heart is for love, and the crown for loyalty. And this was given as a sign of friendship but signified she was willing to consider love if she accepted it.

"Well, maybe not quite engaged but pretty close," he said.

"Shut up, JR," said Devon angrily. "I've only known Eddie for four months. I doubt if he plans to propose to me."

"Why not?" answered JR. "I would."

"JR, quit it. I need to stay focused. I have to call Eddie's family. Will you please stay with my mother and call me if the doctor comes?" Devon put the box back in the plastic bag and placed it by her mother, telling her to keep her eye on it, that she needed to call Eddie's parents, and would be right back. She wondered if her mother heard her, but she did nod her head, so Devon took that as a good sign. She walked out into the larger waiting room, which was empty except for a woman and her child, who was coughing so severely that Devon couldn't imagine what they were still doing in the waiting room. *That child should be getting immediate attention,* she thought. She dialed Eddie's home; luckily Eddie had given her his parents' number if she needed him. His family was great; having a sit-down dinner with all of them was so special. They made her feel so welcome; it felt like she knew them for years. The phone rang several times, and Devon kept thinking, *Please answer the phone.* She immediately recognized the voice on the other end as Michael, Eddie's younger brother.

"Hi, it's Devon. I'm so glad it's you, Michael."

"Hey, Devon, happy holidays. My big brother afraid so far from home that he has to call Mom and Dad again?" He laughed.

"Michael, there's been an accident. My father and Eddie were out on the snowplow this morning, and the truck lost traction because of the icy road. They slid back and overturned in a ditch. My father is in surgery now, and they transported Eddie by helicopter to Albany Medical with a severe concussion. They think his brain is swelling. That isn't good, is it? Please tell me, Michael, is this a serious condition? Why else would they take him to Albany? I'm so sorry, Michael. They just won't give me any information because I'm not a relative. Could you call Albany Med and find out how he is and call me, please, Michael?"

"Listen, Devon, it could be serious, and it could be nothing, but I'll call right now. How's your father?"

"I don't know. We haven't seen the doctor yet. He's still in surgery. We don't even know what injuries he suffered. They had him in surgery before we could make it here. The roads are treacherous, just ice," explained Devon.

"And we haven't had the worse yet. They're predicting a whiteout for here, and it will be moving up to you next. Look, try and stay calm, and I'll get back to you as soon as I find something out," said Michael. Devon said goodbye and returned to her mother.

Another hour went by, and the doctor finally came out to speak to them. Devon's father had a broken rib that punctured his lung; that was why he was rushed into surgery. He also had a broken right arm, a simple break, and a cast was put on it. He was in recovery and should be fine. The doctor said someone would come for them when he was out of recovery and in a room, and he left. Immediately, Devon's mother began to cry. Devon decided to let her cry; that was her way of handling the news. The news about her father was wonderful, and she knew he would be all right, but she was concerned that she hadn't heard from Michael yet. JR had gone down and brought them some fresh coffee, which Devon devoured as hot as it was. She hadn't had breakfast but didn't mention it, or JR would have gone down and brought her something back. As hungry as she was, she knew she wouldn't be able to eat anything. Michael finally called, and the news wasn't good. Eddie had suffered a severe concussion that was causing his brain to swell; they had to drill a hole in his skull to allow the brain room to expand. His vitals were good, but the next twelve hours would tell if they were successful in relieving the pressure on his brain. Michael told her to keep only good thoughts, that his brother was strong, and would come out of this fine. He said he would call her if he got anything further. Devon told him to give her best to his parents. Devon told

JR and her mother, who had finally stopped crying, about Eddie and said that Michael would keep in touch as he learned anything more. After a few silent minutes, Devon's mother told her that she would be fine and wanted to wait for Devon's father to be put in a room, but she needed Devon to return to the lodge and keep things going there. The staff was very competent, but she wanted Devon's presence there in case something went wrong. She knew Devon could handle anything at the lodge.

On the ride back to the lodge, JR asked Devon about Eddie. She told him the truth then added that he was a great guy and she cared deeply for him. He asked no more questions about Eddie but asked about her face. She told him the story of her incident on the subway. All JR could say was that the city was bad news, and she belonged where she came from, right here in the country. The rest of the ride was in silence; that suited Devon fine because she had so much to deal with, and a jealous lover—no, a brother—was not one of them. JR dropped Devon at the side door and told her he was going home to get the other truck. It had chains on the tires and a plow blade on the front. He said he would be back to finish plowing the parking lot. Devon told him to come in after he was done, and they'd have dinner.

Everything was running smoothly at the lodge, for which Devon was grateful. The huge coffee urn in the front of the dining room was full, and a wonderful presentation of cookies, pastries, and cakes lay on trays around it. She checked with the cook, and all was fine in the kitchen. All their employees, however, wanted to know how Warren and Eddie were. Devon told the head of each department all she knew and asked them to pass the information along to any of the others who asked. When everything was taken care of, she ran upstairs to shower and change. Devon waited for JR to finish plowing, and they both sat down to dinner. Devon knew if she left Sunday to go back to school, someone would be needed to remain at the lodge. She knew her mother would insist on being at the hospital most of the time with her father, and there really wasn't anyone else she trusted to maintain order and see that things got done. Dinner was served, and JR seemed especially quiet, pushing the food around on his dish but eating very little.

"Is your dinner all right?" asked Devon.

"What?" he answered.

"I asked if your dinner was all right. You haven't touched a thing," Devon replied. "I can get you something else if you'd like."

"No, this is fine. Just don't have much of an appetite," answered JR.

"JR, it's me, Devon. I know that look. Something's troubling you. What is it?"

"You're going to need someone to look after the lodge when you leave on Sunday, and you are leaving. Your father and Eddie are in good hands, and you need to finish school. You've come too far to quit now," he said. "I don't know much about the lodge, really, but I imagine most of your employees do, and with a little help from your mother, I imagine I'll do just fine," he said.

"You're offering to take care of the lodge?"

"I guess so. Isn't that what family's for?" said JR, looking at his plate instead of at her.

"It's still difficult to think of you as family," said Devon.

"Difficult for both of us, but it is what it is, and you know the Ledger line," he replied, still looking down at his plate.

"Yes, I know it well, and I will do whatever I have to. But know this, JR, I will ask you for your help in running the lodge until my father gets on his feet, but after that, I don't think I can see you. I still love you, JR, and it's way too painful seeing you. I suppose we'll bump into each other from time to time. This is such a small town, but I will acknowledge you just as I do anyone else. I can't keep wanting to run to you whenever I need help or feel sad. It isn't healthy, and it isn't right. Please tell me you'll do the same," said Devon. JR finally looked up from his plate into the eyes of the woman he loved; the woman he would always love.

"It will be as you want it, Devon," he answered.

"I don't want it," she answered. "It's just the way it has to be." JR ate his meal, got a cup of coffee, and asked if she wanted to go back to the hospital.

Getting her mother to leave the hospital was no easy task, but JR convinced her that she needed to stay strong for Warren and therefore needed a warm meal and a good night's sleep. She finally agreed, and on the ride home, Devon told her that JR offered to take care of the lodge until Warren came home. Carolyn didn't say anything but gave a noticeable sigh of relief. When they got back to the lodge, she called the heads of their departments to the office and explained that JR would be staying at the lodge, and any problems were to be brought to him, and to please give him their full support.

19

On the train heading back to the city, Devon reflected on the happenings of the last few days.

Just when I thought he was out of my life, something keeps bringing him back, she thought to herself.

Life could be really cruel sometimes, but she knew what she had to do. She was a Ledger, and Ledgers do what they got to do. Devon decided to take a taxi back to the Stewarts instead of taking the subway; a small luxury, but she was too tired to be brave. A quick trip, and she was home. No one was home yet, so Devon unpacked and made herself some coffee. While she was waiting for it to brew, the phone rang; thinking it probably was the Stewarts, she quickly answered.

"Hello," a man's voice answered; one that she was sure she didn't recognize.

"May I speak to Ms. Taylor?" said the man.

"Speaking," she answered.

"Ms. Taylor, my name is Vinny Sabatini. I believe we have a friend in common, one Edward Griffin or Eddie as he is affectionately referred to, and I have been given a job to make sure you get to school safely each day. You see, I own a car service, and it is my job to get people where they need to be safely and without concern."

"Eddie is in the hospital. There was an accident," replied Devon.

"I am aware of the recent sad event and have sent my good wishes for a speedy recovery to his parents, but that in no way affects the business at hand. What time are you expected to be in school, Ms. Taylor?" continued Sabatini.

"I have to be there by quarter to nine, but I really don't think I need your services," said Devon.

"Eddie informed me that you would resist. I, however, cannot take no for an answer. Am I clear on this issue, Ms. Taylor?" continued Sabatini.

"Yes, and right now, I am way too tired to fight with you. In school by quarter of nine, and out at four thirty," replied Devon.

"Do you have breakfast in, or do you stop someplace before school?" he asked.

"I'm not sure what difference it makes, but I usually just grab a cup of coffee on the way," Devon informed him.

"Did no one ever tell you that breakfast is the most important meal of the day, Ms. Taylor?" said Sabatini.

"Yes, my mother, every day of my life," answered Devon.

"Good for her. Now, your driver will be Sebastion. He is personally known to Eddie and has been with me for many years, but if for whatever reason you are unhappy with him, I will replace him. Now considering the amount of time needed to get downtown and to stop on the way for coffee, Sebastion will call for you at eight ten. If that cuts it too close, we will, of course, adjust the pickup time. If you need to stop at another location, just tell Sebastion when you are picked up, and he will take you wherever you need to go. I realize a car service is new to you, but let me assure you that you will always be safe, and after the incident on the subway that Eddie conveyed to me, I'm sure that is what you want. Am I correct, Ms. Taylor?" he said.

"Yes, you're correct, and thank you for your concern," stated Devon.

"Good, I'm glad we have reached an understanding. If I can do anything else for you, do not hesitate to ask," he said and hung up. Just as Devon hung up the phone, the Stewarts walked in, saying they could smell the coffee in the hall and did she make enough for all? After the hugs and greetings, Devon went to get the coffee, and thinking ahead, she did make a full pot. They told her about their skiing trip, wonderful but exhausting, and asked what Devon had been up to. After hearing of her horrible ordeal on the subway and then the accident, they stopped complaining about how tired they all were.

"My darling," said Mrs. Stewart, "I'm so sorry we weren't here for you. To come back to a cold, empty apartment, how awful." Rory moved over to Devon and hugged her.

"This is all too awful. Is there anything we can do?" she said. Devon, who didn't show any emotion around her mother, broke into tears, thanked her, and said the only thing she was worried about right now was Eddie.

"I'm sure the doctors are taking the best care of Eddie, darling, and knowing Eddie, he will come out of this just fine," said Mrs. Stewart. "If there's anything, anything at all, that we can do, you have to just ask."

"Thank you, but I'm fine, and Eddie has taken care of my going to school without having to take the subway. As I was giving my report to the police, he arranged with a friend of his who owns a car service to pick me up and bring me home from school."

"That's what I like about the boy, levelheaded in an emergency. Good for him, and lucky for you," replied Mr. Stewart.

Yes, thought Devon, *lucky for me.*

After coffee and more stories about Mark's crazy antics on the slopes, they called it a night. Devon got into bed, pulled the covers over her head, and kept saying, "Please let this all just be a dream."

Devon's first day riding to school in a chauffeured car was most uncomfortable for her. She was so used to doing things for herself, and that this felt wrong somehow, but it did give her time to reread the last chapter in her book. The next few weeks were to be all hands-on work. She tried so hard to concentrate, but her thoughts kept coming back to Eddie.

"Sebastion," said Devon, "tomorrow, could you pick me up earlier, say seven thirty? There are some dear friends I need to tell about Eddie's accident. They're in the flower district, West Twenty-Seventh Street, Nardell Brothers'."

"I know them well, and I will be happy to do it. Eddie is a favorite of many people, including myself," answered Sebastion.

"Yes, I'm finding that out." The next day, she told Raymond and Kevin about Eddie's accident and promised to keep them informed of his progress, and they also made her promise to have breakfast with them before school ended. She promised she would.

The three weeks leading up to Christmas were just a blur. Eddie was released from the hospital two weeks after the accident. Physically, he was fine but still had no memory. Devon stopped by to visit the family and Eddie, but he had no idea who she was. The family was grateful that she came by; they liked her from the first day Eddie brought her home. She stopped by again just before she left to go home for the Christmas holiday. She had gotten gifts for all of them. Mrs. Griffin gave Devon a package before she left and told her to open it when she got home. With Christmas on a Thursday, she would have a long weekend at the lodge. The Stewarts' house was like a Christmas wonderland with decorated trees in every room. Since Devon would not be with them, they decided to have a special dinner and exchange some of their presents on the twenty-fourth. It was so wonderful of them, but it meant that she would have to leave late to catch the train to Hudson. Sebastion let her off at Penn Station, and she told him that she would call to tell him what time she would return from the Catskills. As he helped her with her bag, she handed him a small gift. She could see that he was definitely caught off guard; he muttered a thank you and jumped back into the car. Devon laughed as she watched him quickly pull away. The train was full and on time when it reached Hudson, and she was so happy to see that one of the workers from the lodge was there to collect her and not JR. The lodge looked beautiful as it always did, especially at Christmas with all the bushes covered with lights and the tall spruce tree in the center of the lawn fully lit and decorated. The inside was all right; not as good as she would have done. Decorating the lodge at Christmas was one of her favorite things to do, and she went all out. Fresh arrangements with boxwood and fir greens in all the rooms and garland of pine hung everywhere; and there were three large trees, one for the lobby, the dining room, and the lounge, all decorated with a different theme. Her father was doing so well, and except for the cast on his arm, you wouldn't know what he had gone through. Her mother looked tired, caring for her father and seeing to the lodge. Even with JR's help, it had been difficult, but with Devon home for almost four days, she should be able to get some much-needed rest.

Oh, it was so good to be home, she thought, and then she saw JR. Her father was home now and doing well, so why was he here? Devon was exhausted after her long day. She kissed her parents, picked up her bag, and said she was going to sleep, and they could catch up in the morning. She showered, unpacked her bag, and finding the gift from Mrs. Griffin, she sat on the bed and opened it. It was a picture of Eddie. His wonderful smile, the twinkle in his eyes, and that look of happiness he always had on his face. Devon left her bedroom for the playroom she had taken Eddie to. She put the back halfway down on the lounge chair, held the picture to her chest, and cried as she gazed out the large windows. She remembered Eddie saying how it looked like something from a fairy tale, but there was no fairy tale here, just cold reality. The weekend went by so quickly, and she didn't want to leave, but she had to. She only had three weeks left of school, and then she would be home. How good that sounded.

Devon was invited by Mrs. Griffin to dinner on New Year's Day. She had spent New Year's Eve at home alone at the Stewarts, watching the ball come down on TV. They had all gone to some elaborate party and begged Devon to come with them, but she refused. Mark even offered to get her a date, but she still refused. There was nothing to celebrate. The day at the Griffin's was pleasant enough, and Eddie seemed to be more at ease with her, but still no recognition. She left feeling a little deflated; surely he must have some memory of her.

She was surprised to get a phone call from her father on Thursday, telling her that she needed to come home on Friday evening. He wouldn't explain why, just that he needed her home. All she could think about through the night and in school on Friday was that there was something wrong with her father or mother, and it was so bad they didn't want to tell her over the phone. The train ride to Hudson and the ride to the lodge seemed to take forever, but she was finally there and ran into the lodge to confront her mother and father, pleading for some bit of information for why she was called home. Devon's father had someone take over the desk while her mother got them coffee and brought it into the office. Devon didn't want coffee; she wanted answers but accepted her mug anyway and drank it, patiently waiting for someone to say something. Having ran out of patience completely, she blurted out that she knew it was bad news, and they might as well get it over with. If one of them was ill, she wanted to know about it now. Her father assured her that they were both fine, and what they had to tell her was not about them; it was about her. Devon's father was rather stern at this point. He told Devon he would tell her everything and did not want her to open her mouth at all until he was finished, and at that time, he would answer her questions. She agreed and he began.

"Right after Thanksgiving, Russell Ledger died," said her father. Devon began to ask what it had to do with her. Her father put his hand up, and she quickly stopped. "As I was saying, JR's father died, and JR insisted we were not to tell you. He didn't want you anywhere near the man when he was alive and certainly not when he was dead. There was no honoring this man. Back in August, when you found out what Ledger did to your mother and that he was your father, you told JR. You told him that you were his half sister. We know the feelings you had for him and watched you agonized over it, but what we didn't know was how JR dealt with it. When you left his house, the first thing he did was get a drink, then he got down his revolver, and went up to the big house. He went to confront his father. His father was in the study with his mother. He asked his father if it was true, about the rape, about everything. His father told him to get out, but his mother screamed at her husband and told him to tell the truth for once in his life. She said it was all true. That's why she left his bed twenty years ago when she found out there were all kinds of young girls parading through the house. Some consented to sex, others he forced himself on like Carolyn. She said she should have done something then, but she didn't want a scandal. She had always protected the Ledger name. She went on to say that the girl they paid off to leave town was also not JR's fault. It was his father that did it. JR said that now he knew why his father was always asking him to bring his friends around, especially the girls. His mother said she bought a condo in Florida near her sister and was leaving in the morning. She saw the gun that JR had and begged him not to shoot his father, that he wasn't worth going to jail for. Better to leave the gun and pray he use it on himself. She gave her son a kiss goodbye and left to finish packing. That's when things really heated up. His father called him the vilest names and said he was no son of his, but JR kept calm. He knew the only thing his father valued was power, and the power came from his massive wealth, so JR knew right where to cause him the most pain. He had his father write a new will. JR dictated what was to be in the will. His father refused at first, but JR told him that he always ruined his life, and that loving you and finding out that you were related left him nothing to live for, and that he had no problem pulling the trigger. His father complied and wrote out the will, then JR made him write another note, turning over the running of all the Ledger business and the control of the money to his son, with a note that he was suffering from mental disabilities. JR had him call his attorney and tell him to come right over. His attorney was there within the hour, and his father explained what he had done and wanted him to witness and affix his seal to it. The housekeeper also witnessed the signing. Then JR made sure he took the papers instead of his father's lawyer, who would have destroyed them if his father directed him to. After everyone left, JR placed the bottle of bourbon in front of his father with two glasses. He filled his father's to the top and said that they should celebrate the downfall of Russell Ledger. His father picked up the glass and threw it at JR. Luckily, it missed, and JR just got another until his father finally drank it. JR said, 'It was nice doing business with you,' and left, leaving the old man downing his drink and pouring himself another. The next part is one I know will be upsetting, Devon, but please let me finish. JR went home and thought about using the gun on himself but talked himself out of it. If he couldn't have you, he could always be there if you ever needed him, and my accident proved he did the right thing. He poured himself a drink and drank straight for four days, not eating or sleeping. His farm manager found him lying on the kitchen floor and called the family doctor. The doctor wanted to put him in the hospital, but JR refused to go. With the manager's help, they got him cleaned up and put to bed. The doctor got the necessary equipment, and he hooked him up to an intravenous bag to help him get some fluids in him and to balance his electrolytes. He also gave him some vitamin B to help with the alcohol. The two men stayed with him for two days until he could get up and try to eat something. At first, all he did was throw up but eventually managed to keep food down. His manager stayed with him for a few more days with the doctor paying daily visits. JR recovered, but the doctor said that if his manager hadn't found him, that he would have died there on the floor. When he recovered and realized what he had done, he vowed to never drink again, and as long as he has been here with us, he never has. Without his help, Devon, I don't know how your mother and I could have handled everything. We owe him a great deal, and now to your part. Tomorrow morning is the reading of the will, and you are named in it. JR didn't go into specifics, just that you're in it. So tomorrow we will go to the lawyers. I promised JR that I would go with you to keep my hand over your mouth, if necessary, when the lawyer reads the part concerning you. He knows you would try to refuse anything left to you, and he said he wanted to make sure you get your dream, and that this would help. All right, I'm finished. Any questions?"

Devon looked at her parents, began to say something, but instead she ran out of the room. Her mother started to go after her, but her father held her back. He told her to let her go, that it was a lot to take in, and Devon needed to find the strength to work it out for herself. Devon flew up the stairs to her room; she closed the door behind her and stood shaking. So many things were going through her mind, too many things. Her mind was overloaded with thoughts and memories. She had to hold on to the bed to stop the room from spinning. Suddenly all the hurt and disappointment, the things that would never be, and the love she would never have come flooding in like a massive storm. Devon had reached a breaking point. She stood trembling, then with one swoop of her arm, she knocked everything off her dresser. The collection of snow globes her father started to give her when she was ten, the little ceramic piggy bank she made when she was in Brownies, the small wooden jewelry box that held a locket her parents had given to her on her sixteenth birthday all went flying. She turned and did the same to the wardrobe; then she pulled down all the curtains, her rage just beginning. The shades came next, then on to the closet; she pulled every piece of clothing off its hanger, then the hangers themselves went flying. She was exhausted, but the rage wouldn't let her stop. She pulled the blankets and sheets off the bed and even lifted the mattress off its frame. When there was nothing else to destroy, she just stood in the middle of the room that looked just like a cyclone had hit it; and in a way, it had. She began to feel calm. Devon never knew where she found this calm, but in times of crisis or extreme difficulties, somehow, eventually, it showed up; a preservation mechanism of sorts. Devon reached down and grabbed her comforter and a pillow and opened the door just as her parents were about to come in.

"Would you see if housekeeping could straighten my room please," she said. "I'll be sleeping in my hideaway room. Please wake me early enough to get a shower in the morning before we have to go to the lawyers, Dad. Good night." And off she went through the door to her special room, not saying another word. Her parents looked at what she had done to her bedroom. There wasn't one thing standing in its original spot. Carolyn turned to Warren and began to cry. Warren held her softly, letting her get it out. When he thought sufficient time had gone by, he took her by the shoulders, told her to pull herself together, and that they had a room to straighten.

The following morning, as the sun came up, it shone so brightly through the large picture window. With no shades or drapes, its bright light woke Devon, who got up thinking to herself that she just had the best night's sleep in ages. She walked quietly to her room, not sure of the time and didn't want to wake her parents. Her room had been put back the way it was before the earthquake hit. Most things survived, but some did not. Two of the snow globes were missing, but something had to take the hit for the home team, and they were it. She found something to wear and lay it on the bed, then quickly showered and dressed; for some reason, she was starving. She opened the little wooden jewelry box and took out the locket with her mother and father's pictures in it and put it on. She had chosen to wear black woolen slacks and a two-piece matching cardigan sweater set in dusty rose, and the locket looked perfect with it. She finished lacing her suede shoes, straightened her pants so the center seam fell precisely in the center of the laces, and left her room. She saw her mother and father at their usual table, having breakfast. She walked into the kitchen and emerged a few minutes later with a plate piled high with pancakes and bacon. She stopped by the coffee urn, filled a mug, and continued on to her parents' table.

"Who do I thank for picking up the pieces of my room?" she asked.

"Ah, that would be your mother and me," said her dad.

"Didn't want the staff to know your daughter lost it last night," she said as she shoveled some food into her mouth.

"Something like that," replied her dad.

"Warren!" exclaimed her mother.

"It's all right, Mom, really. Thanks for the cleanup in aisle three. Looks like a few snow globes didn't make it though," she answered.

"Snow globes can be replaced, but how about you?" asked her father.

"I'm fine. The realization that this chapter of my life has ended and not the way I thought it would was extremely unsettling, but I'm all right with it now. Now that it's really over, I can look forward to the next chapter, which hopefully will be a lot more fun," answered Devon as she polished off the last of her breakfast then got up to get more coffee. She asked if either of them needed a refill, but they both declined and watched in amazement as their daughter walked to the coffee urn with all the confidence and maturity she ever showed. Her parents looked at each other and didn't know whether to laugh or cry. Devon walked back to the table and sat down, took a sip of the hot coffee, and said to her parents that they looked like they just saw a ghost.

"I'm not quite certain what to say to that, Devon," said her father. "You're handling this awfully well."

"Yes, I am. Last night was a different story, but this is a new day, and I plan to handle it incredibly well. JR put himself through hell for me, and I want him to know that with his help, I will make my dream come true. Anytime you're ready, Dad. We don't want to keep the lawyer waiting." Devon got up to get her coat, and Warren gave Carolyn a kiss on the cheek. She asked her husband if he thought their daughter was really all right, and Warren gave her another peck on the cheek and told her not to worry, and that Devon found her strength.

The drive to the lawyer's, which Warren expected to be a quiet one, was anything but. Devon said that Russell Ledger had been a rich man, and with JR's help, she might get a nice slice of the pie. And that whatever it turned out to be, she would use it to remodel the flower shop once she finally took it over, which wouldn't be until March 1. But it was quickly approaching, and Devon had so many ideas about the remodel. Her father suggested they had an architect look at it for any structural changes she might want and help her with any other ideas, and Devon happily agreed that would be the plan.

Besides Devon and her father, the only other people attending were Mrs. Ledger, JR's mother; JR; and the attorney. The attorney went through the will quickly, explaining each part and how it pertained to each of them; all the while noticeably glaring occasionally at JR, and JR just smiling back. When it was over, Mrs. Ledger told Devon that she hoped she could find it in her heart to forgive her for not having the strength to stop that evil man (meaning her husband) years before he could hurt so many people, JR included. Devon said she knew she thought she was doing the right thing in trying to avoid a scandal to blemish the Ledger name, and she felt only sorrow for her part in having to live with it on a daily basis, and that she hoped she would finally find some peace and enjoy her new life in Florida. Devon was surprised when Mrs. Ledger kissed her on the cheek and whispered in her ear that she would have made a great Ledger. She kissed and hugged JR then left the office in tears, saying she was sorry over and over. All eyes watched a very sad woman leave the office. All the money and land she was to receive seemed to mean nothing to her. When she was gone, Devon went to JR; with her father standing behind her, she extended her hand and said, "Thank you, JR."

His answer was typical JR.

"You do what you can." He smiled. "You know the Ledger line."

"You do what you got to do," they both said in unison, leaving her father wondering what they were talking about. But he kept quiet. This was a moment for them.

"Maybe one day you can do something for me." JR reached down, kissed Devon's cheek, left, and didn't look back. The ride back to the lodge was totally silent this time. As her father looked over at his daughter, he thought to himself that he never saw her look more beautiful than right now, and he knew Devon would be better than ever.

20

SCHOOL FINISHED WITH NO big graduation party, no fanfare at all, just a certificate stating that she was now qualified to handle the grooming of different dog breed types. As they walked out the door, the next class was walking in. Well, she could cross off one more thing from her list.

Since school finished on Wednesday, she thought she could get to see Eddie and his family before she returned to Catskill. She called Mrs. Griffin and was immediately invited to dinner on Thursday. She spent the rest of Wednesday packing up her things in a box to mail home. The Stewarts were very busy with their practice, plus the wedding they were planning for Rory. Rory and Mark decided not to wait until they graduated law school and wanted to get married now.

The wedding would take place after they finished the semester, so they were leaning toward sometime in July. Rory insisted that if she decided to have bridesmaids, she definitely wanted Devon to be in the bridal party. Devon was thrilled and said she would be honored. The Stewarts were sad to see her leave, especially Mr. Stewart. He said that she was the only one who gave him a tough game when they played chess. She even beat him once, which took him by surprise. They left the board sitting up in his study; and either of them, when they had time, moved their piece, leaving a note that they had done so. Mr. Stewart got into the habit of immediately checking the board game before he did anything else.

Mrs. Stewart often got angry when he was called for dinner and was hung up on his next move. Devon begged them to please let her give them something for letting her stay with them for the six months, but they refused, saying it was such a pleasure having two daughters in the house; but they did say that if they found time, they would come up to the lodge before winter's end to get in some skiing. Devon told them that they would be her guests no matter what time of the year they could come. Hugs and kisses all round, then goodbye. The same at the Griffins: dinner, hugs and kisses, and promises to come by anytime. Devon hugged Eddie, who, by now, looked forward to her visits. All the sisters and Michael, Eddie's brother, said they would stay in touch and would call if there was any change in Eddie. One last thing to do, and she was on the train home. A small gift of $300 for Sebastion for making her life so much easier traveling around the city. At first, he refused, claiming he was well compensated by his employer, Vinny Sabatini, but Devon insisted. She also called Mr. Sabatini to thank him for his wonderful employee and once again asked if she could pay the bill for his services; but again, Sabatini refused, saying it was taken care of. Devon wondered how. Eddie hadn't worked since the accident in November. She told him she would be honored if he would like to spend a weekend at the lodge as her guest. He gave his thanks, said goodbye, and hung up.

"Your boss is a man of few words, I take it," she said as she was getting out of the car for the last time. Sebastion said he was, but he had the look that spoke for him. He helped Devon with her bag and wished her well and said if she ever needed him again, he would welcome the chance to be her driver. Devon thanked him and was lost in a sea of people walking into Penn Station.

21

DEVON WORKED DAILY IN the flower shop, giving Mrs. Ogden some much-needed time off. Even with the new girl she hired, she was doing most of the more expensive arrangements, but Gloria was getting better, and she liked to do all the things Devon didn't like: answering the phone and taking orders or waiting on people in the front of the store. No, Devon would rather be behind the scene, invisible, doing what she loved: working with the flowers and taking a seemingly unrelated bunch of greens and flowers and turning them into something breathtaking. Her eye for color and form outdid anything Mrs. Ogden ever achieved, and customers were welcoming her return with increased orders and insisting that Devon made all their arrangements. Devon resumed her Monday morning trips to New York to pick up the flowers for the week, and her visits to Nardell's always ended with a quick sit-down with the brothers for bagels and coffee and some light banter. They always asked about Eddie, but Devon had nothing new to tell them, which made them sad, especially Raymond, who had grown so attached to him. A quick "give your parents our regards and our blessings on you," and Devon was off to a few more stops. The Nardell Brothers' carried all the basic flowers a shop depended on but not the exotics that Devon had been using more and more. Imports from South America, strange pods and other strange grasses, and orchids of the most unusual varieties and spectacular colors. Shopping was a little more expensive, but she was making it up in the prices people were willing to pay for the most beautiful or unusual. All the arrangements at the lodge had been completely discarded, and new ones took their place. Her parents never knew what to expect when they came down in the morning. There was always something new. They were worried that she was working too hard; with the shop, the lodge, and her trips every few weeks to see Eddie, they barely saw her. They were lucky if they sat down to dinner with her once a week. They both agreed they needed to talk to her about reinstalling the custom they had of having dinner together as a family each night. Devon used to love those nights; they hoped she still did.

Devon promised to have dinner with her parents at least three times a week, which was more than they hoped for. They desperately missed her company, and her mother just wanted to make sure her daughter was eating enough, for it was not unlike Devon to forget about eating when she was engrossed in her work. She and her father spoke to an architect about the remodeling of the store, and he promised to have some possibilities for her to look at by the end of February. Devon was to take over the store March 1 and had planned to close for a few weeks to get the updating done, but business was doing so well that if the remodeling could be done at night, she wouldn't have to close at all; however, finding a contractor who would work at night was pretty slim. Still, she was confident she would find someone even if she had to pay extra.

Devon seemed down one night at dinner. When her mother asked her what was wrong, she said she didn't know.

"I know this may sound strange since our time together was so short, but I really miss Eddie, the real Eddie before the accident. Does that sound dumb, pining for a man you only spent a few months with?" asked Devon.

"No, dear," replied her mom, "Eddie was a larger-than-life character, always full of happiness and laughter. Watching the two of you together on Thanksgiving was so special. You seemed to be one person at times, saying the same things, ending each other's sentences. And the way he looked at you, the love was so evident. So no, Devon, it's not dumb at all."

"You know, I only spent a few hours with the guy, and I miss him," said her dad. Just as Devon was convinced her father was teasing her and was about to tell him to stop, her cell rang. She excused herself from the table to take the call, and as if the powers that be had heard her silent plea to have Eddie back, the person on the other end of the line was Michael, Eddie's brother.

"Devon, hi, it's Michael," he said.

"Michael, is everything all right?" stammered Devon.

"Yeah, it's all fine. How about you?" he asked.

"Busy. The shop is really doing well. I barely have time to take a breath. Why, what's up?"

"The strangest thing. The other day, we had snow. It wasn't much, but for a while, it covered everything, and Eddie kept sitting by the window, watching the snow fall and saying that he wanted to go to the fairytale land. Any idea what that's about?" asked Michael.

"Oh my god, Eddie and I watched the snow fall when he came for Thanksgiving. We were by a huge picture window, and everything was white, and all the little white lights we have around just about everything here made Eddie say that it was magic, a fairytale land," answered Devon. "Do you think he might be remembering?"

"I don't know, but I think it's a good sign. That's why I'm calling. My sister Kathlyn, you know, the nurse, thinks it might be a good idea to bring Eddie up to the lodge. That's why I wanted to know if what he has been saying meant anything. Now that we know it does, I think it's worth a try. I know it's the last weekend in February, and you're probably swamped with skiers, but in case you had any empty rooms, Kathlyn, Judith, and I would bring Eddie up. What do you think?" asked Michael.

"Michael, that would be fantastic. I can't believe it. My mother and father and I were just talking about him at dinner. Hold on, Michael, let me get to the desk and check the reservations." Devon ran to the desk as her parents looked on, wondering who was on the phone. Devon quickly flipped the pages, ran her finger down the page, and gave out a small "Yes, thank you, God."

"Michael, we're in luck. We do have some rooms available. When did you want to come up?" she asked.

Kathlyn has a late shift, so we couldn't leave until Saturday morning," said Michael. "So we would just be there overnight, Saturday," answered Michael.

"Michael, I'm so excited. I can't wait to see you guys. It seems like an eternity since I saw you all last. Wait till I tell my parents. Do you know how to get here? I can give you directions," said Devon.

"Thanks, but we got directions off the computer. I remember passing your exit when we went up to see Eddie in Albany. So we're okay there. Just wanted to be sure you had room for us," replied Michael.

"If we didn't, I would have to lose someone's reservation." Devon laughed.

"Well, I'm glad we don't have to resort to that. All right, Devon, we'll see you early Saturday afternoon. There's no snow in the forecast, so we should have smooth sailing. See you then."

"Don't stop for lunch. We'll have it ready for you here. Bye, Michael," said Devon as she ended her call then spun herself around like a top. She started to run to her parents' table, but with all the people milling about, she decided she should walk or they would think her crazy, and she was crazy with excitement. She slipped into her seat saying nothing. She picked up her fork and began to eat when her mother asked if everything was all right. Devon was trying so hard to remain calm.

"I just had to make a reservation, that's all," answered Devon.

"Oh," said her father, "who's coming? If it's those damn Donalsons with those brats, I swear this time I will throw them out. I promise you."

"No, you won't have to worry about this bunch. They're well-behaved," said Devon, who couldn't hold back any longer. "That was Michael. He and Kathlyn and Judith are bringing Eddie up for the weekend!" she screamed. "Can you believe it? We were just talking about him. Michael said Eddie has been saying some things and wanted to know if I recognized any of it, and I did. When Eddie was here for Thanksgiving, it was late, and I took him to my special room. As we watched the snow fall, Eddie said it looked like a fairytale land. Michael said Eddie has been sitting at the window, watching the snow fall down there and saying over and over that he wanted to go to the fairytale place. So they thought by bring him here, he might remember more. Even his doctor thought it might help him remember. Oh god, I can't wait. Now I have to call Mrs.

Ogden and see if she can cover for me on Saturday. I want the day off, and there isn't anything special going on, so she should have a slow day. I better do that now."

"No, you can finish your dinner and call her when you're done," said her mother.

"All right, all right," said Devon as she began to wolf down her meal.

"Devon," said her mother, "some manners please." Devon finished her dinner and even had coffee.

"Mom, I think we should have turkey and apple pie. The same dinner we had when Eddie was here. Can we do it?" asked Devon

"I don't see any problem with that," answered her mother.

"Great," said Devon as she excused herself from the table and went to call Mrs. Ogden. She already decided that if Mrs. Ogden couldn't come in, that she would just have to close the store for the day. On Friday, she would just have to call any client who was picking up arrangements on Saturday and see if they could get them on Friday, telling them that some emergency came up and she had to close on Saturday; but after listening to Devon, she said of course she would come in and for Devon to make the most of the weekend. She knew how this separation was affecting Devon. Devon always threw herself into her work when she was sad and would work until she exhausted herself. Mrs. Ogden prayed that something good would come out of this visit.

On Saturday morning, Devon ran about, making sure the rooms were just right. She put fresh flowers in all the rooms and had to straighten everything even though housekeeping was just in there. Then she went into the kitchen to check on lunch. The chef told her that if she came into the kitchen one more time, he was going to lock her in the freezer. Her parents forced her to sit and have breakfast. It was only eight thirty, and this was going to be a very long morning. By eleven, Devon was a basket case. There was just no calming her. She saw Michael pull up to the door, and she ran out to greet them, telling Michael to bring the bags in then please park a little farther up so as not to block the door. As soon as Kathlyn and Judith got out of the car, Devon was there to greet them with hugs and kisses. She was so grateful that their family was like hers in that no one ever arrived or left without hugs and kisses all round. Devon helped the girls carry the bags inside then waited for Michael and Eddie. When they finally appeared, Devon hugged Michael then went to Eddie.

"Hi, Devon from the Catskill," he said. Devon stopped dead in her tracks, looked at Michael, then rushed into Eddie's arms.

"I'm so happy to see you, Eddie. You look great. Did you enjoy the trip?" Devon wasn't sure just how personal she should make her conversation with him and decided to let Eddie take the lead.

"The trip was nice," said Eddie. "I didn't realize how far from the city it was. It's beautiful here."

"Michael, did you have any trouble finding us?" asked Devon.

"No, I had my pilots in the back seat yelling out directions," replied Michael.

"And if it weren't for us, where would you have ended up? Go ahead, tell her, smarty," said Kathlyn.

"I think we were headed for Catskill by way of Connecticut." Judith laughed.

"All right, enough busting on the driver. Devon, this place is amazing. I can't wait to see the rest of it," said Michael.

"Thank you. Why don't we take your bags up, and you can freshen up, and then I'll give you the grand tour," said Devon as she picked up one of the bags and led them up the staircase to their rooms. She left them there to settle in and joined her parents in the dining room.

"Michael and his sisters look very much alike, don't they? Do they take after their mother or father?" asked her mother.

"I think they resemble their father more than their mother. Even Patricia looks like the father. Eddie is the only one who looks like their mom. He always used to joke and say they got all the brains from their dad, but he got his charm from his mom."

"Who's got all the charm?" asked Michael as he and Eddie were approaching.

"That's what Eddie used to tell me. He said you got your brains from your dad, but he got his charm from your mom," answered Devon, smiling. "Right, Eddie? You got your charm from your mom."

"And my smile." Eddie laughed. "And you got yours from both your parents. They are always smiling."

"Mom, Dad, this is Kathlyn, Judith, and Michael, and of course you remember Eddie."

"How could we forget Eddie? It's so nice to see you again." And they gave him a small hug. "Kathlyn, Judith, Michael, welcome to the lodge and our home. Please sit or have you been sitting too long? I know that trip seems longer and longer each time we go to the city." Devon's father got up from the table to greet everyone and shook hands with them as they were presented.

"I'm so glad you could make it. Devon prayed all week that we wouldn't get any snow to postpone your trip," he said.

"We did too," said Judith. "I've never been out of the city except to go to Jersey, and that's not really out of the city. That's why when I pick a college, it's going to be as far from a city as possible."

"Don't let her fool you. One look at a big bug and she'll be screaming for Dad to come and get her," said Michael.

"Will not," answered Judith.

"Okay, children, I for one could die for a cup of coffee please," said Kathlyn. "Then Devon is taking us on a tour."

"Please, help yourselves. Devon will show you to the coffee urn. It's filled all day and night, so feel free to help yourselves anytime. At lunch and dinner, we have a very nice selection of goodies too," said Carolyn. "Would anyone like something other than coffee?" To which all answered no and followed Devon to the coffee urn.

"Wow, I've never seen such a huge coffeepot," said Judith.

"When the lodge is full, that's anywhere up to thirty-five people, not counting kids, then there's the staff and anyone else that drops by to say hello, and this urn is always the center of attention," said Devon, leading the way back to the table. When everyone was seated, Michael began a conversation with Devon's father about the construction of the lodge; and the girls began speaking to her mother, leaving her and Eddie by themselves. At first it was a little awkward trying to find something to talk to Eddie about; then she decided to ask about his parents to get them started.

"I miss your parents. How are they?" she asked.

"They're good. They miss you too. They told me to give you a kiss for them," answered Eddie. "Ready?" And Eddie kissed her cheek. Devon's immediate reaction was to touch the spot he kissed.

"Thank you, and when you go back, you can give them a kiss for me, okay?" said Devon.

"Then you had better give it to me so I can pass it along," said Eddie, smiling from ear to ear.

This is the Eddie I know, she thought to herself. *Please, God, let him remember something, anything, please, especially for his family.* Devon desperately wanted to say, "Make him remember me, just me," but she knew that sounded selfish and stopped herself. Devon gave Eddie a long kiss on the cheek, and Eddie did the same thing. He touched the spot she kissed. Devon thought she saw recognition in his eyes, but it was just wishful thinking. When everyone had finished their coffee, Devon took them for a tour through the lodge. Everyone marveled at how large and beautiful the lodge was. Judith asked if Devon did the entire flower arranging for the lodge, and Devon answered that she did, and that she changed them throughout the year to reflect the seasons. Kathlyn remarked that she wished they had time to see the shop, and Devon told her that after lunch, she would love to show them the shop. She explained how she would be remodeling it as soon as she officially took it over on March 1. She told them about the architect she hired to figure out not only the shop but the adjacent building, which she wants opened up to the flower shop, and that it would be a pet shop and grooming salon, and that the upstairs was being converted to an apartment where she would live for a while. Kathlyn and Judith said at the same time that they were sure it would be wonderful, and with Devon's talent, it would be the best flower shop and pet store around. After lunch they were all going down to see the flower shop, except for Eddie, who was complaining of a severe headache. */9Michael told Devon that he had been having them for the past few weeks and was supposed to get a CAT scan next week. He gave Eddie his pills and walked him to their room. After making sure he got into bed, Michael joined the others. Michael said the pills usually kept him out for a couple of hours. Devon asked them if they would rather wait and see the shop tomorrow and stay to make sure Eddie was all right. Kathlyn agreed that they should stay with Eddie since he was in a strange place. He might wake up and panic, so they decided to wait until Sunday to see the shop.

The rest of the afternoon was spent sitting in the lounge, talking or playing pool. Michael first took on his sister Judith, who he beat easily. Kathlyn was slightly better, but Michael soon beat her, but after losing three games to Devon, he quit and proclaimed her the victor. They all laughed at Michael. It was not easy for him to admit defeat.

Devon took them upstairs to the area that overlooked the pond, where several people were ice-skating. Judith asked if it was difficult to ice-skate, and Devon asked if she would like to try. They usually had a few pairs of skates around. The three of them headed out for the pond with Kathlyn staying put. She was not eager to go out in the cold and wanted to wait to see if Eddie woke up. Judith's attempts to skate proved too difficult for her, and she spent most of the time on her bottom, but it did make for some deep belly laughs. All she wanted to do was to get back to the lodge to warm up. Once they returned to the lodge, Judith went up to her room to change her wet, cold clothes. Michael, always looking for competition, started a game of chess with Devon's father; while Kathlyn, Devon, and Carolyn enjoyed another cup of hot coffee and indulged on some incredible nut cookies. Conversation covered Kathlyn's nursing position, to how their father was coping with his back injury, to the history of the lodge. Judith joined the women after getting herself coffee and was asked what field of study she had in mind when she graduated high school in June. She admitted to being undecided. She knew she didn't want to go into medicine like Michael and Kathlyn and certainly would not follow Patricia and go into real estate, no matter how much money she was making. Judith liked to write and was considering journalism, but just what kind, she didn't know. Mrs. Taylor embarrassed Devon when she told them how Devon had one dream her entire life and worked constantly with that one goal in mind.

Kathlyn said, "Knowing what you really want is half the battle, and working at getting it was the other half." She said she knew she wanted to be a nurse when one day when she was around ten they found a baby bird and they couldn't find the nest it fell out of to put it back, so Kathlyn took it upon herself to care for it. With her success came the realization that nursing was for her. Judith made faces and claimed barf pans were definitely not for her. Evening soon approached, and Warren and Michael were still at it at the chessboard. Carolyn reminded them that dinner would be served in one hour, and they had to have a champ by then.

Dinner was wonderful; the chef did exactly as Devon wanted it. Devon had told the girls earlier that she had the same meal prepared as the one they shared on Thanksgiving, hoping it would seem familiar to Eddie. Eddie awoke in plenty of time for dinner and watched Michael and Warren conclude their game of chess with Michael the winner. Warren told Michael to never play with Devon, or he would realize how much he didn't know about the game. She was an extremely formidable opponent. Michael said he knew that after getting whipped in a few games of pool. Eddie laughed and said Devon was good at everything, even hurting bad guys. Michael and Warren looked at each other but didn't question Eddie about what he said. The doctor said to just let him say the things he remembered without questioning anything he said, which was so difficult. Everyone sat down to dinner at six, and suddenly all the little, white twinkle lights that were strung over the draperies came on. They came on earlier in winter because it got dark so early. In summer, they didn't come on until eight. Eddie stopped eating and said the lights made it seem like a fairytale place, just like he kept saying at home in the city. Everyone glanced at each other, not sure what to say, except Judith.

"You're right, Eddie. It does look like a fairytale place. It's so pretty here with the snow."

"Yeah, I love it here. Maybe I'll move here," he said.

Michael started to say something about who would run the business but stopped after Kathlyn nudged him. Dinner was leisurely, which the girls said they loved; at home, everyone was coming or going, so you barely had time to catch up on the latest events. Soon after coffee and dessert, Eddie got up and took Devon's hand and told everyone that they would be right back. After they disappeared around the corner, comments on the meaning of that were exchanged.

"I guess we'll just have to wait and see," said Devon's father. "Let's hope it is something good."

Eddie walked up the stairs with Devon in tow. As they reached the landing, Eddie went immediately to the door on the left, opened it, and Devon closed it as she came through. They walked down the short hallway, and Eddie opened the next door that led to Devon's special place. He closed the door once Devon was through, leaned against the door, and pulled Devon back to him. He wrapped his arms around her and kissed her over and over. When they parted, Eddie took Devon by the hand to sit on the lounge chair. He put the back down, placed one arm behind his head, and with the other, held her close.

"I love this view," he said. "I want to stay here and watch the seasons go by, just you and me."

"It's a lovely thought, but we'd never get any work done," she answered.

"What about all the little fairies? Don't they work any other time of year besides winter?" he asked.

"Maybe they do. Maybe they can do all the work for us. Then we could watch spring come with all her fresh light-green colors, then watch as the green grows deeper and most of the flowers are blooming in summer, then autumn with all the fabulous reds and yellows, and that would bring us right back here to winter," replied Devon.

"That works for me. How about you?" But before Devon could answer, he rolled toward her and kissed her longer, deeper this time. Devon closed her eyes and relaxed against him. His kisses were passionate, unlike she ever received from him, and she kissed him back with the same passion. They stayed that way until Eddie pulled away blushing.

"What's wrong?" asked Devon.

"The little man downstairs has awakened. See what you do to me. Another cold shower night," he said. At first, Devon wasn't sure what he meant, but when he mentioned a cold shower, she got it and buried her head in his chest and felt his embarrassment but couldn't let it go.

"So you're telling me that this has happened before?" she said, trying to hold back the laughter.

"Oh yeah, been there. Done that. And I'll tell you, cold showers are not at all comfortable," he replied.

"Well, do they relieve the problem?" she said mischievously.

"Not even a little bit," he said emphatically.

"I'm so sorry." She chuckled.

"No, you're not. I can tell you're enjoying my pain," he said.

"Okay, maybe just a little." Devon glowed. She wished they could take it to the next level, but she had to know how Eddie felt when he found out about the accident. She kissed him and told him how much he meant to her and debated whether to tell him now or not. This was probably the best opportunity to tell him about the accident.

What to do? What to do? she said to herself. Finally, Devon made the decision. She would tell him.

"Eddie, there is something I need to talk to you about, and it's serious," she said.

"Wow, it must be serious. You just lost your happy face," he answered.

"Eddie, today's date is February twenty-sixth, two thousand nine. It's not Thanksgiving in two thousand eight. The meal was what we served on that day because we thought it might help you remember what happened back then." Eddie put one hand up to his temple and began to make small circles with his fingers. "The night I brought you here in this room, it was snowing. It snowed heavily all night, and after we had breakfast, you and my father took out the snowplow and began plowing the parking lot. Then you drove down to the pond to make a road for the skaters. On the way back, the roads were so slippery from the freezing rain that the truck was unable to maintain traction and slid backward and flipped over in a ditch. You cracked your head on the door, and Dad's seat belt came undone, and he slammed into you. The police and paramedics came as soon as they could and got Father out on a backboard, and with help, you climbed out yourself. You both were taken to the hospital. By the time Mother and I could get there, my father was in surgery. He had a broken rib that punctured his lung and a broken arm from trying to grab the steering wheel so he wouldn't hurt you. When I asked how you were, they told me that you had been taken by helicopter to Albany and were in the head trauma unit. You had a severe concussion, and your brain was beginning to swell, and that they had to drill a hole in your skull to relieve the pressure. I couldn't get there. The roads were too dangerous." Now Eddie was rubbing both temples, and Devon could see the change in Eddie's face. He had lost color, his face was a pasty white, but Devon continued anyway. "After a few days, the swelling subsided, and you were going to be fine. The only problem was that you lost your memory, not of just the accident but everything. Michael and Kathlyn brought you home after two weeks in the hospital, and you have been living at your parents' for the last three months. It was difficult at first because you didn't even remember your family, but gradually it got better. You were more comfortable with them. I visited you as much as I could, but you never remembered who I was, and I kept coming down to the city as often as I could after I graduated from school. The last few weeks, Michael said that you were experiencing headaches and would say things that no one recognized like the day it was snowing and you said it looked like a fairytale land. That was exactly what you said when I brought you here for the first time. It was snowing, and all the little, white lights were on, and you said those exact same words. When Michael told me what you said, we decided that if you came to the lodge then maybe you would remember something." Now Eddie was becoming highly agitated and holding his head in pain. Devon didn't know what was happening but thought she had better get Michael. As she left the room, she could see Eddie rocking back and forth, moaning and massaging his head. Devon left the room and ran downstairs to find Michael and Kathlyn. She found them in the lounge, sitting on the low lounge seats in front of the fireplace. She quickly told them what she had done and asked them to come with her to Eddie. They ran up the stairs and down the hallway and into the room where they found Eddie sitting up and holding his head in one hand while leaning on the other. Michael was the first to get to him.

"Eddie, what's going on? Devon said you had a headache. Are you all right? Do you want a pain pill?"

"Hi, Mikey, I'm fine. The pain was pretty bad for a while, but it's almost gone now. I think a few Tylenol will do the trick," said Eddie.

"Devon told me this incredible story, and suddenly flashes of light, bits of pictures were all flooding my mind. It started a few weeks ago when the headaches started. I sensed something wasn't right, but I didn't know what. I thought they were just leftover dreams or something. It was like a big puzzle that was missing half the pieces, and the harder I tried to make sense of it, I got those pounding headaches. How's Mom and Pop? Are they all right? I bet I was a big pain in the ass to live with, huh. Never mind, I don't want to know. Where are my lovely sisters?" Both Kathlyn and Judith ran and sat down next to their brother. The four of them held each other; all of them in tears, as was Devon and her family. It was Judith who spoke first.

"Eddie, you remember everything, don't you?"

"Yeah, Button, I remember everything," answered Eddie. Button was the name he sometimes called his baby sister; always saying she was cute as a button and pinching her cheek.

"Well, that's one thing you could have forgotten, but it's okay. I don't mind. In fact I really missed you calling me that but not the cheek pinching," said Judith, all the while holding her brother as close as she could. After a minute or two, Michael said he wanted to give Eddie a quick once-over. He checked his pulse then directed a small light into his eyes. When he was satisfied nothing was wrong, he asked Eddie to stand up and see if he felt any dizziness. Eddie did as asked and said he was fine. Michael checked his eyes once more. When he finished, Eddie turned to find Devon. He opened his arms to her, and she walked into them. His arms surrounded her and pulled her close. He kissed the top of her head, holding it with one hand. Devon looked up lovingly at him and kissed him gently.

"If I had caused you more harm, if I did anything to make it worse, I just can't bear to think about it. Tell me you're all right. Please just tell me you're all right," said Devon. Eddie held her close and promised her that he was all right. Then he thanked her for having the courage to tell him the truth. If she hadn't taken that chance, he would still be struggling to put the pieces together. There was not a dry eye in the room, and that included Devon and Eddie.

"All right, everyone, why don't we all go down and have a nice cup of coffee. I for one could use something a little stronger right now, but I'll settle for coffee. Who's with me?" said Devon's father.

"Make mine sweet with two Tylenols please, bartender." Eddie laughed.

"Eddie's back. Eddie's back. Eddie's back" was all Devon heard. It was all she needed.

They all walked back down to the dining room, and Mrs. Taylor asked, "Who's up for some goodies, pie, pastries, or cake?" Then she said never mind that; she would just bring some of everything out. Everyone filled a mug with hot coffee and returned to the table where they ate dinner. Everyone was talking. It was doubtful if they heard any part of conversation, but it didn't matter at all. Eddie was back. That was all that mattered. The girls said they wanted to call their parents, but Eddie said that they would be sleeping by now, and he wanted to be the one to tell them when they got back to the city. Everyone was exhausted, but no one left to go to bed. They were all on a happiness high and knew they couldn't sleep now anyway.

The morning found everyone down early for breakfast, and the mood was definitely different than when they arrived. Everyone was enjoying breakfast, chattering away and extremely happy, especially Devon. After breakfast Devon's father took Eddie and Michael down to the road to see where the accident happened, but Eddie still had no memory of it. He said it didn't bother him that he couldn't remember it, and Mr. Taylor said he wished he couldn't remember it either. It was no fun, he said. Once they got back inside, the girls were ready to take a ride to see the flower shop. Michael and Eddie got a takeaway cup of coffee because they were chilled from standing outside. Devon pulled up with the large van, and everyone climbed in it. She took them on a short scenic ride around Catskill then went to the shop. Judith said she never saw so much open space before; miles of just empty land and few houses.

"Duh, that's why they call it the country," said Michael.

Devon opened the front door, and everyone went inside to look around. The first thing Eddie wanted to see was her heating and air-conditioning system. Devon told the others to look around while she and Eddie went into the basement. Michael decided to tag along with them, not particularly interested in the flowers. Devon showed Eddie where the furnace was, and it was just like he had been working every day with no time lost. He was on top of his game as always. He explained to Devon that she really needed to consider another form of heating source, and that the one she had was old and not energy efficient, especially if she expected to use the same unit to heat the other building where the pet store would be. Eddie checked the duct work and the electric panel box, both sorely outdated. After checking everything downstairs and walking through the shop, Devon told him where she wanted to put a refrigerated display unit; the old one was way too small. Eddie moved on and checked the rest of the store out, then the greenhouse part where Devon explained she wanted to keep it cool in summer to grow plants and just a tad warmer in winter so she could keep seasonal flowers like poinsettias for Christmas and already greened up containers, making them ready for the flowers.

Next, Eddie wanted to see the building next door. Mrs. Ogden had rented it out to an antiques dealer who left some six months ago, and the store had been empty since then. Eddie said that at least someone had the good sense to keep the heat on. He checked all the wiring that he could see and went down to the basement, checking everything there. Devon explained how she wanted each area set up, and Eddie told her what kind of outlets and such that she would need. The furnace and duct work were worse than in the flower shop. Devon was becoming discouraged, saying she had no idea it was going to require so much more work than she anticipated. She figured she might as well show him the upstairs where she wanted to make an apartment where she could live for a while until the stores started making a profit. She estimated she would have to live there at least three years; then she could rent it out and buy a house. And she wanted a small greenhouse so she could grow orchids and a few other specialty plants. She followed Eddie through the space and showed him where she thought the kitchen and bath could go and the wall that would need to be taken down for the bedroom. Eddie didn't say much; just did the uh-huh thing. Michael didn't say anything either. Devon guessed he probably didn't have a clue about renovating anything anyway. He never worked in the business like Eddie, and his father insisted he go right from high school to college and med school. Michael probably never lifted a hammer, but she trusted Eddie's judgment completely. Eddie said he saw everything he needed to see and would like to see the architect's plans, which were back at the lodge. The girls were still looking at some of the silk flower arrangements when they got back down into the shop. Devon told them to pick something their mother might like so they could bring it home. Both girls resisted at first, but both girls agreed that their mother would love the arrangement in pinks and lavender. They were her favorite colors. Devon thought she should have remembered that from her visits to their house. There was a lot of pink and lavender scattered about in glass vases, fancy bowls, and the mauve-colored carpet that ran from the dining room into the living room. The girls picked an arrangement they all agreed their mother would love, and Devon wrapped it; then it was back to the lodge. Eddie pored over the architect's plans with Devon; Michael and Devon's father were looking on also. Eddie made a few suggestions that seemed to work better than what was in the drawings. Devon told Eddie to make the changes in pencil and write the description of the changes. They would decide on the final plans when they reviewed them with the architect. Having finished going over the plans, lunch was served; and since both Michael and Kathlyn had the eleven-to-seven shift at the hospital, they wanted to leave right after lunch. It was sad seeing them go, but Devon knew she would be seeing them again. She promised she would try to come down in two weeks on Sunday.

22

ON MONDAY MORNING, DEVON made her usual trip to New York to pick up her flowers for the week. She told the Nardell brothers the good news that Eddie had regained his memory; they were thrilled and would give him a call. On the trip back to Catskill, it began to rain. Devon listened to the weather, and there was no prediction of any freezing rain, for which she was so grateful. The trips to New York seemed liked they were getting longer and longer. She wished she could find someone reliable to make the trips for her. Back at the shop, the flowers were cut and put in the walk-in cooler, and Devon began making the orders for the day. The girl that Mrs. Ogden had hired, Gloria Knowles, was working out just fine. She opened the shop Monday mornings and cleaned the pots, getting them ready for the new flowers. She also did very well in taking orders and putting together small arrangements. Mrs. Ogden also had a man who regularly delivered pieces for her, and he also was doing a good job. Devon needed to find another person to work in the shop; she would teach her what Gloria already knew. During the holidays, she would need more help, and she knew she couldn't always count on Mrs. Ogden, who was now retired and planned to travel. With the money Devon just inherited, she wasn't worried about paying someone; however, the business had picked up, and she was sure at this point she wouldn't have to touch the money just yet, leaving it for the remodeling she knew would cost a considerable amount.

On Tuesday, they got hit with two funerals. The funeral sprays and other pieces had to be at the funeral parlor by four, so Gloria greened up the pieces, and Devon put the flowers in. With so many pieces ordered for one person from family and friends, it was hard to try to make them all look different; but when they were done, Devon was very satisfied that they all turned out well. Wednesday was a slow day, and Thursday proved to be a surprise. Gloria walked into the work area and told Devon that a customer would like to place an order but would only place it with her. Devon couldn't imagine who was insisting on her, but when she walked out, she couldn't believe her eyes.

"Eddie, what are you doing here?" she said.

"I'd like to place an order, please," he replied.

"An order? An order for what? what are you doing here?" she asked again.

"I told you I want to place an order. Do I have to get the other girl back, or will you take it?" answered Eddie.

"All right, all right, I'll take it. What would you like?" asked Devon.

"I would like one dozen long-stemmed yellow roses, please," he said.

"One doz yellow roses. Got it. Would you like these delivered, or will you be taking them?"

"I'll take them, and I would like a card to go with them," said Eddie.

"Here is our selection. If you would care to make it out, I'll put it in the box," said Devon.

Eddie picked a card and wrote, "Dear Devon, sorry I missed your graduation. Love, Eddie." He then placed it into an envelope and handed it to Devon. Devon took the card and returned in a few minutes with a long box with a bow tied around it.

"Here you are, sir. That will be twenty-five ninety-two," said Devon as she took his money and rang it up on the register and gave him his change and said, "Thank you."

He asked if she would give him directions to the lodge as he wasn't sure he could find it. She told him she had deliveries going near there. If he cared to wait, he could follow the delivery van. Eddie said that would be fine; he would wait. After a short wait of fifteen minutes, the delivery man explained to Eddie where to turn off after following him, and off he went without saying goodbye. Devon was worried that maybe he lost some of his memory again. She couldn't wait until it was four o'clock. She asked Gloria to close up because she had something to attend to. Devon drove quickly to the lodge, curious to see what Eddie was doing. She found her parents and Eddie at the table, having coffee. As she walked by the desk, she was told there was a delivery for her; one look at the box and she, of course, knew what they were. She opened the box, took out the card, and asked the girl behind the desk if she could find a vase to put them in. With card in hand, she approached the table.

"Now do you want to tell me what the hell is going on?" she yelled at Eddie.

"Devon, please lower your voice," said her mother. "And is that any way to greet a guest?" Devon shook her head and left to get a cup of coffee from the urn. When she came back to the table, she calmed herself and asked Eddie what he was doing here.

"I had to come back, Devon. This is where I want to be. Here with you. I want to do the renovations on the buildings. I think I'm the best qualified and understand what you want, plus I can get all we need from my contacts in New York, and it will save you a lot of money," he said.

"But what about your business in the city and your family?" asked Devon.

"I had a long talk with my parents, and Dad said that Geo was doing a good job with his help. And my mother said that I should be where my heart wants to be, and that's here with you. I had my CT scan Monday, and everything is fine. I worked Tuesday and Wednesday, but I knew it just wasn't what I wanted to do anymore. I want to be here with you, helping to make your dream come true," answered Eddie. He was so serious but smiling all the while, trying to be brave in case his plan was rejected.

"Did you two know about this?" she asked her parents.

"No, of course not," said her father. "We're as surprised as you are, but it's a wonderful surprise if you ask me. We have been going over the architect plans again, and I think Eddie has some brilliant suggestions. You really need to take a look at them."

"I will, Dad, but first I would like to speak to Eddie alone. Eddie, would you come upstairs please?"

"Sure, Devon," replied Eddie as he put down his cup. He followed her upstairs to the special room where they had privacy; no one ever went into the room except Devon.

"All right, tell me what's going on?" she said. Eddie explained that it was just as he said downstairs; he wanted more than anything in the world to be here with her and to work on her building.

"I know how I feel about you, Devon, and I understand if you don't feel the same way about me. We lost a lot of time after my accident, but I want the chance to begin again. And as for your building renovations, I am the best choice. I can handle the heating, air, and refrigeration. That's what I do, and I'm good at it. You will have to get an electrician for all the new wiring, I'm not licensed for that, and a builder who can replace the old windows and insulate and put up siding on the outside. The rest I know I can handle with just a helper. If when the place is done and you don't want me, then I'll just go back to my old life, and you won't see me again. But I need a chance, Dev," pleaded Eddie. Devon turned her back to him. In that moment, everything they had together before the accident, how he handled everything when she was attacked on the subway, getting her the car service, calling her just to see how school was going, listening to her go on and on about the things she planned to do, never once telling her it couldn't be done; and just when she was sure of her feelings for him, the accident happened. Yes, they did lost time, but she knew without a shadow of a doubt that now that he had regained his memory and was the same Eddie, all the feelings for him were still there and even stronger. She loved him. Devon turned back around, and Eddie saw her tears. Inside, his heart felt like it stopped beating. He gently wiped the tears from her face.

"I guess I know the answer," he said.

"No, you don't know the answer, you big jerk," said Devon. "I love you so much, Eddie. I can't tell you how many times I thought of asking you if you ever would consider living here with me, leaving the city and your family. But I know how close you all are, and I thought it was to selfish to ask you. But if this is truly where you want to be. You're sure. No doubts. Then yes, this is where I want you to be, with me."

Now it was Eddie's turn for tears, and Devon gently wiped his away. Then they both started to laugh and hug and kiss. Eddie took the claddagh ring from his pocket and asked her if she would wear it. He told her that it just meant that she was willing to consider love, nothing more, until they spent more time together and knew without question that they belonged together. Devon put the ring on her right hand, with the crown pointing away from her heart. "Let love and friendship reign forever." That was the meaning of the ring. Love and friendship, they had in abundance.

"Come on. My parents must be biting their nail by now," said Devon. After a few long and tender kisses, they left to seek out Devon's parents. Devon's dad was pacing back and forth, and her mom was staring into space. As soon as they saw Devon and Eddie returning, Devon's dad sat down, picked up his coffee cup which he had already emptied, and tried to look very nonchalant.

"Oh, back already," he said.

"Yeah, like you haven't been sitting on the edge of your chair wondering what was going on," answered Devon.

"Yes, I'll admit we were a little curious," replied her father. Devon asked Eddie if he wanted coffee and returned with two mugs. They sat down slowly, sipping their coffee until Devon's mother couldn't stand the suspense any longer.

"All right, you two, you've made us sit and squirm long enough. Now for god's sake, please tell us what's going on," she pleaded.

"Eddie needs a room and three squares a day," said Devon.

"Oh, Eddie, have you been kicked out?" asked Devon's mother.

"Good god, man, what happened?" said her father. Devon looked at Eddie and said she thought they better tell them before one of them had a stroke. Eddie laughed and shook his head.

"Where to start," said Devon. Devon finally told her parents everything, and they couldn't have been happier. Devon showed her parents the claddagh ring Eddie gave her and explained it was not an engagement ring but close to it, and that would probably come when the building was finished, especially the apartment upstairs. Devon's father said this was time for a celebration and asked one of the waitresses to bring them out four wineglasses and a bottle of Asti Spumante, which was Devon's favorite. With glasses filled and raised together, Warren wished for much happiness for Devon and Eddie.

23

THE PLANS WERE FINALIZED. Eddie's ideas would work out the best. And as Devon left for New York to pick up the flowers, Eddie began rechecking measurements and writing down a list of equipment needed for the job. Devon's father called the electrician and the contractor that worked on the lodge when they did their remodeling; both were on board for Devon's place. They planned to meet with Eddie to see what needed to be done and when work could be started. Eddie was in his element, and it felt good. The flower shop was finished first because it was only cosmetic work inside: mirrors, new paint, shelving, new counter for order taking, and base cabinets for additional storage. A little tweaking to the work area with more base cabinets for storage and additional shelving for orders to be delivered, and the first part of the remodeling was done. Once the pet store was opened up and the wiring done, the heating units and duct work in the basement would be put in place. Work was progressing nicely with little or no surprises. Eddie said that sometimes when you began pulling down walls in an older building, things were not always as they should be, but they were lucky up to this point. The real challenge would probably be upstairs. Eddie traveled to the city twice to pick up needed items, stopping off at his parents for just a few minutes each time. They were well but missed him. Eddie missed them too. After a few weeks, Devon said they should take a few days off. Mrs. Ogden would cover the shop for Saturday, and Devon would pick up the flowers on Monday as usual, but the rest of the time would be her and Eddie's. She told her parents that she and Eddie were going to the city and planned to leave Friday night, right after work. They wanted to spend some time with Eddie's parents and would be back on Monday with the flowers and a few other things Eddie needed.

Eddie thought a few days off was a great idea, and he wanted to be able to spend a little more time with his parents. Devon took the van, and they left early Friday afternoon. They drove as far as Newburgh, where Devon got off the thruway and pulled up in front of a motel. Eddie asked Devon why she stopped, but Devon just told him to wait in the van and that she would be right back. It never occurred to Eddie that Devon had plans she hadn't discussed with him. Devon returned and drove around the building. Getting out, she grabbed her overnight bag and told Eddie to grab his. Devon opened the door to a room and set her bag down. Eddie did likewise, waiting for an explanation.

"I know you're wondering what we're doing here, but I thought that you and I could use some private time together," she said as she put her arms around his neck. "Very private time. We stay overnight tonight, and maybe tomorrow night, drive to the city early Sunday morning, spend the day with your parents, stay overnight, then leave early Monday morning to get the flowers, and back to Catskill. What do you think? Want to spend some private time with me?" Eddie was so surprised. He couldn't think of anything to say except thank you.

Finding out that Devon was still a virgin surprised Eddie. He asked if she was sure this was what she wanted, and she told him that he was the person she was saving herself; a little lie, but the fact that she wouldn't still be a virgin if the truth didn't come out about JR being her half brother was something she didn't feel was necessary for him to know. She just said that she was glad she waited.

The weekend proved to be perfect. Eddie was gentle but passionate and not a disappointing lover. Meals with Eddie were always fun. He made her laugh through every course, and he was a little old-fashioned. He opened doors and pulled out her chair.

He did all the little things she was beginning to love. She told him he would have to be patient with her, and that she was so used to doing all those things for herself. Trying to make fun of the situation, Eddie told her that if she wanted, she could open his doors. His male ego could take it. Devon couldn't help wrapping herself around him and kissing him and asked him why he was always so sweet. She asked Eddie if this was what love was, and he said loving was easy, but living could be hard. And the more you were considerate and kind to your partner, the easier life would be. He admitted he got that from his mother when he told her that he loved Devon.

"You have a very wise mother, and I will thank her when I see her tomorrow for the sweetest and kindest man I've ever known."

"Okay," said Eddie, "but tonight, you can thank me and love me again."

Eddie's parents were thrilled to see Devon. She told them about all the wonderful work Eddie was doing in the store. She told them that the suggestions he made would save both time and money and how her parents were so captivated by him. Mrs. Griffin was so excited to see her wearing the claddagh ring and immediately had to tell the rest of the family who hugged and kissed her and welcomed her into the family. A few others of Eddie's aunts and uncles were called and invited to dinner to meet Devon. The little dining room was wall-to-wall Griffins, and everyone had advice to give. Dinner lasted all evening, with more coffee, desserts, and an abundance of laughter. Eddie wasn't kidding when he told her that the next morning, her sides would hurt from laughing so much. She could barely bend over to brush her teeth the following morning when they were getting ready to leave. Her sides hurt so badly. Eddie's mother and father insisted on getting up with them even though it was five thirty. Devon said they could get something to eat at the diner on the way, but Mrs. Griffin would hear none of it. She prepared eggs and bacon for breakfast. It was difficult saying goodbye. They had been so wonderful. Devon had to wonder if Eddie was having second thoughts about living upstate with her, but as soon as they got in the van, he said, "No, he wasn't having second thoughts."

Devon looked at him totally surprised and asked him how in the world did he know what she was thinking. He said it would be what he would be thinking if the roles were reversed. Each day, Devon learned something new about Eddie. He wasn't just a big man with a huge smile and twinkling eyes. He was way more complicated and wiser than she ever imagined.

The Nardell brothers were so happy to see Eddie; they hadn't seen him in over five months and were thrilled that he was with Devon. They both were a little surprised that he had decided to give up the business to live upstate with Devon but wished them both much luck and made Eddie promise that he would occasionally come down on Monday with Devon. Raymond, who was always closer to Eddie, insisted they come a little earlier so they could share some breakfast. He promised he would. The van was full of flowers, and they said their goodbyes. Eddie said he hadn't realized they missed him, and Devon told him that he was the kind of person you didn't easily forget.

With the pet store finished, Eddie prepared to tackle the upstairs while Devon interviewed people to work in the pet store. She found two that she was satisfied with, and they began putting items in their place. She had stickers placed under the hooks so they knew where to put everything. She and Eddie had put in the glass aquariums and decided what fish they would start with. She didn't want to go overboard and buy too many uncommon varieties just yet. The shop looked great, and they had a small celebration to announce its opening. The business was slow to start, but after a few weeks, it really picked up. Eddie was halfway through the apartment remodeling and ran into a few problems; nothing major but things would have to be repositioned slightly. Another few weeks, and it was complete. He hadn't allowed Devon to come upstairs for the last few weeks; he wanted her to wait until it was done. The new stairway that led from the back room, where arrangements were held until delivery, led right up to the kitchen. No more having to go out of the store to the doorway next door to go up to the apartment; and the other door that led down to the street in the front was off the small foyer as you came in to the living room. Eddie came down and told Devon that she could come up the back stairs now. Devon had been trying to get a peek for days, but Eddie always caught her and chased her back down. Devon expected it would be just fine but wasn't prepared for the transformation. A few weeks ago, it was just a boring dead space, and now it was incredible. Eddie was right. He did know what she wanted, and it was perfect. Devon walked through all the living space, checked the closets, the bath, and the kitchen, then told Eddie it was truly miraculous, and she loved all of it.

"Now there's only one thing left," she said.

"What's that?" replied Eddie.

"We have to go shopping for furniture and curtains and stuff," she answered.

"I think you had better take your mother with you for that. I'm no good at that stuff," he said.

"I can't take my mother. I need the man I plan to live with in this apartment to help me pick things out. After all, he has to like where he's living, doesn't he?" said Devon. "Eddie, I know this is backward, but will you marry me?" Eddie just stood grinning from ear to ear, nodding up and down, because he was speechless.

When he finally could speak, he said, "Okay, but no frilly stuff in the bedroom."

The wedding was planned for September, Devon's favorite time of year. It would be held, of course, in the lodge, and Devon's parents were accepting no reservations for that weekend except family. The wedding was going to be simple, with all of Eddie's relatives there. Even his father planned to make the trip with a little help from some strong painkillers for his back. Their honeymoon would have to be short because business in both shops was getting better and better, and both of them were needed to work. Eddie and Devon's life settled into a routine. She worked in the flower shop most of the time, and he sometimes made deliveries for her now that he was beginning to find his way around the area. Eddie also worked in the pet shop, taking care of the fish and tanks. They finally found a woman who had a great deal of experience grooming dogs, and the grooming salon was finally opened. Devon's plan was right on track. Just one thing was weighing heavily on her mind, and she asked her parents what they thought she should do. They told her to listen to her little voice. It always steered her right. Somehow, Devon knew that was what they would say, and it was what she decided even before she asked them.

The next quiet evening they had, Devon decided to tell Eddie everything. JR, her mother's rape, and all she was left in the will thanks to JR. Eddie listened attentively until she was done. He never said a word. Devon told him that she loved him, but if he wanted to change his mind about marrying her, she would understand. Eddie excused himself and said he needed to get some fresh air. When she heard the door close, Devon thought she had lost him. She called her mother and told him that Eddie left. Her mother tried to console her, but Devon hung up the phone and curled up in a ball on the new couch they bought. It had been Eddie's choice, and now she would be sitting on it alone. Devon didn't cry. She went over all that she just told Eddie. It would be a lot for anyone to take in. Eddie drove around for a while. Then found himself outside JR's house. He sat in the car, thinking of what he wanted to say to this man, if anything. He finally got the courage to knock on the door. When JR answered, he didn't look surprised. He told Eddie to come in and asked if he wanted anything. Eddie said no, and JR asked him to come into the living room and followed behind him. JR sat down facing Eddie.

"This is a little awkward," said Eddie, but Devon told me all about you and your father and the money from your father's will that you were responsible for. "She loved you, and it hurt listening to her, but she had the courage to tell me everything, and I think that she will never be quite over you, but I know without a doubt that she loves me, and we are going to be married and hopefully have lots of kids and a long life together, but if something ever happens to me, I expect you to be there for her as her brother."

"Before you showed up at my door, I used to wonder how I would feel watching her marry and live a happy life without me, but I don't feel sad anymore. It took a man with great understanding, a man of great heart, to come here and face me as you have. I think Devon's got the man who couldn't be better for her, and I know you will be the one to make all her dreams come true. I believe I can look at her now and see my little sister. Thank you, Eddie, you're a good man."

"If you don't mind, JR, I think we should keep this little talk just between ourselves," said Eddie.

"I think you're right on that one," said JR, escorting Eddie to the front door and stood until he saw the last of his taillights disappear. *Good for you, Devon. Good for you*, JR said to himself as he fought back the tears.

It was just before midnight when Eddie returned. Devon was still in the same position she was in when he left. Eddie went into the kitchen and made a pot of coffee; after it brewed, he brought two cups into the living room, giving one to Devon, whose first thought was to refuse it but thought she should take it since he went through the trouble of making it. He sat down on the couch next to her and sipped the coffee. Eddie asked her again how much land and money she was left, and again she told him. She could tell that he was thinking hard about something, but she couldn't guess what.

"You're probably wondering what I'm thinking about all this," he said.

"Of course, I'm wondering. I know it's a lot to take in," Devon replied.

"Everything we seem to do is a little backward. I know I'll never make more money than you, and I'm okay with that. I don't have a very big ego to worry about. I'm just trying to decide if I should start my own business like I had in the city, or if we should start the no-kill animal shelter now instead of waiting three years, and that maybe we should build our house now so that when you get pregnant you won't have to go all through that, and we could just rent out the apartment," answered Eddie. "What do you think?" This time it was Devon who was speechless. She couldn't believe her ears. This man looked past the money, past everything she told him. Another man might not have taken all the news as calmly as he did, but he was not like any other man. He always looked forward toward what could be. He never saw the negative, and helping her make the rest of her dreams come true was all he lived for. He loved her that much.

"How many kids are we having?"

"Oh, two might be nice. Three is not good. The middle child always gets overlooked, so it's two or four," Eddie said seriously.

"All right," said Devon. "Do you want to start now or wait till our honeymoon?"

"Let's see. The wedding is only a month away, so I think it's okay to start now, and you probably won't even have to alter your wedding dress, and lots of babies come a little early." He laughed as he picked her up off the sofa and carried her to the bedroom.

Eight months after the wedding, Devon gave birth to a beautiful baby girl. Emma, for Eddie's grandmother, and Carolyn, for Devon's mother. Emma Carolyn Griffin was brought home from the hospital and placed in her own room decorated with horses and carousels. The five-bedroom house drawn by Eddie and Devon was large but not overly so. Landscape materials were picked out by Devon, and the enclosed and heated in-ground pool was perfect for swimming through the winter. The only small problem was Emma. She was a colicky baby and was up almost all night, crying. Devon was exhausted, so they agreed to hire a pediatric nurse for the evenings so Devon and Eddie could get some sleep. At three months, she did a complete turnaround and began sleeping through the night. The nurse was no longer needed, but a suitable nanny had to be found because both the flower shop and the pet store were so busy. And Devon was especially needed in the flower shop. Customers still requested Devon to handle their business for weddings and casket sprays. Through a friend of her mother's, a nanny was found that Devon and Eddie felt comfortable with, and she could start immediately. With that problem solved, they were back on track.

24

WHEN THEY RETURNED FROM their honeymoon, Eddie had decided to start his own business. One of his men from the business in the city, Aaron Hartwell, who had worked for Eddie for over five years told Eddie that if he ever started a business in Catskill to keep him in mind, and that he would like to get his family out of the city and raise them in the country because the city was getting more dangerous with murders, muggings, and robbery. Aaron and his wife had three children ages nine, five, and one year old. Eddie was more than happy to have Aaron work for him; he knew the work as well as Eddie. Devon found them a house to rent, and they moved up to Catskill, and Aaron began working for Eddie. After working in the business for a little more than a year, Eddie grew restless. Devon knew something was wrong, but Eddie kept telling her everything was fine and not to worry, but things weren't fine. Eddie just wasn't himself. Finally one evening when the baby had gone to sleep early, Devon made coffee, brought him a cup, and asked him what was wrong. It seemed everything they started or needed to talk about happened over a cup of coffee. Eddie finally admitted he wasn't happy and hadn't been for a while. Devon's first thought was that he had grown tired of her, but Eddie quickly assured her that wasn't it. He loved her more now than he did before, if that was possible. No, the trouble was work. He just wasn't enjoying it as he used to. He loved checking over the situation, deciding what needed to be done, and even figuring up the material needed for the job. He just didn't like the actual physical end of it anymore and wasn't sure what he should do. He told Devon that he never thought about working with fish and animals, but after doing so for a few months, he missed it. The thought of a no-kill shelter had been on his mind for a long time, especially since he spoke to people who came into the pet store and told him how many dogs and cats were euthanized every year. He said it hurt his heart thinking about it. Eddie said, in the city, most people he knew never owned a dog because most didn't have a backyard for them. He knew a few people with cats but not dogs, and the strong connection he felt to the dogs that came in the store made him want to pursue a new path. He told Devon that he hadn't told her before because he was afraid that she might not take him seriously.

"This big dumb guy from the city wants to take care of dogs. How crazy is that?" said Eddie.

"Don't do that. Don't ever do that with me," replied Devon. "You're not a big dumb guy. You're incredibly talented and sensitive, and everyone adores you. You connect with people so easily, Eddie. Everyone always asks about you, and why would I laugh about you working with animals? I've never seen a dog come into the shop that you didn't immediately established a rapport with. You calm them so easily, and we have had some mean dogs in the store, yet they are no compliant with you. You definitely have a way with them, and we can't ignore that. If you feel that is what you want to do, then we will start planning the shelter."

"I could still go to new jobs and figure everything up and hire a helper for Aaron, and he could do the rest. I know Aaron would work fine on his own," said Eddie.

"Eddie, you've made me so happy, given me your support, picked me up when I was feeling down, gave me the encouragement to go on, and I want you to do whatever it is that will make you happy. I love you, you know that, and we'll do whatever you want," replied Devon.

"I think this is it, Devon. I know this has always been a dream of yours, too, and I don't know why, but I think this has been mine ever since you told me about the dogs and cats that were put to sleep every year. I want to work with the animals that have nowhere to go," he answered. "Are we still good moneywise? I don't know what it will take to get started. I know with the remodeling and building our house we must have gone through quite a bit," he asked.

"We don't have to worry about money. The stores are making a profit, and there's rent from the apartment, and we haven't put a dent in my inheritance, so let's get started. I thought the flower shop and pet store was my dream, Eddie, but that was before I met you. You are my real dream."

After Devon and Eddie viewed the property and sat down and drew the plans for the various enclosures, work began. Wire fence was placed around the entire acreage then divided into smaller sections. The large barn that Russell Ledger kept his horses in worked out wonderfully in the plan. The first two stalls would be totally enclosed, and a door would be put in the rear with a smaller door in it so the cats could come and go. The area would be fenced in with a wire roof so no cat could escape over the fence. Scratching posts, climbing trees, and diagonal boards would be affixed to the inner walls so the cats could walk to any level they wanted, and of course there would be multibaskets for sleeping. When it was complete, the sign would read "Kitty Korner." The last four stalls would be left for horses and storage. The largest area next to the horse lot would be for the dogs. Devon knew they would be coming in multitudes. People who bought puppies, thought they were cute until they grew up, and they no longer saw a cute dog, just worked. This was the only building that had to be built. A place large enough so dogs could come out of the extremely cold weather in winter. Plenty of individual doghouses were also placed around the back of the building, filled with straw and a woolen door cover for winter. Many breeds preferred to remain outside in winter, but small dogs needed to be kept warm. The dog area was named "The Bark Park." The clubhouse where Ledger entertained his fox and hound riders was perfect for an office, an area for the vet to work in, and an isolation room when new animals were brought in. They were inspected, neutered or spayed, and given their immunization shots before they could be released into the general population. Building the sanctuary was a large undertaking, but Eddie loved every minute of it, even the time it took to build a pond so the dogs could cool off in the summer heat. The sign over the new facility read "Griffin No-Kill Animal Sanctuary." Eddie wanted it to be Devon's name first; after all, it was her idea and it was, but she knew without a doubt that this would be where Eddie found his niche. When it was completed, he was filled with excitement waiting for their first guest. He was even more excited when Devon told him that they would be having an addition to their family as well.

The first guests arrived in the first week they opened: two old cats whose owner had to go into a nursing home and a very large dog, battered and broken. Word soon spread of the sanctuary and dogs, cats, and a horse were dropped off in the first month. Eddie hired a man who knew a little about horses but would work in all the areas cleaning and feeding. When he wasn't looking at jobs and estimating cost and materials for his heating and air-conditioning business and instructing Aaron the best way to install the units, Eddie could be found at the sanctuary. A man who had never been near a horse in his life or in and around dogs, Eddie had an uncommon ability to communicate with them. Dogs and cats arrived weekly; dogs with collars that were so tight it grew into their necks, dogs that had been tied to trees with little food or water and no human contact, cats with burned hair, animals so covered with fleas and ticks they barely had enough blood left in them to live—these were what Eddie dealt with every day. His amazing commitment to these poor animals astonished everyone except Devon. There was so much love in this man, and the animals were so much better for it. He could not get used to the cruelty humans inflicted on animals. The worst of these, he never told Devon about. Now that she was in her eighth month, he didn't want to cause her any undue stress.

This pregnancy was proving to be a difficult one, and she only came into the flower shop to work for weddings or when she was asked for specifically; otherwise she stayed home to rest. The latest wedding was an extremely lavish one, and she and her staff worked late on Friday; everything had to be delivered early at the hall, and Gloria was going along to get the table arrangements in place. They were just finishing up when loud thunder could be heard, and flashes of lightning were playing with the lights. They got out the flashlights and a few candles just in case the lights went out and they were in the dark for a few minutes before the generator could kick in. Eddie called Devon and told her he was coming to pick her up. He didn't want her driving alone. He helped her into the van, but she couldn't get comfortable. She was having some pain. Eddie said they were going directly to the hospital to have her checked out and preceded in that direction. The rain was coming down so hard he could barely see the road; the wipers were useless. After turning onto the road that led to the hospital, a huge tree lay across it, knocked over by the strong winds or helped by a hit of the lightning. Eddie had to turn around and find an alternate route; Devon told him which road to try but by now was in extreme pain, crying that the baby was coming. Eddie knew that the road took them right past the Ledger house; with no lights on in the bungalow, Eddie drove past it and up to the big house where he could see many lights on. He pulled into the circular driveway, jumped out of the van leaving Devon, and started banging on the door. The housekeeper answered, and Eddie asked if JR was at home. She said he was, and Eddie ran past her, yelling to JR. JR was in the study and came out when he heard the racket. Eddie told him about Devon, and they both ran out to the van. JR told Eddie to bring her into the house and instructed the housekeeper to make up the bed in the small guest room on the ground floor. Eddie picked Devon up, trying to be gentle. She was in so much pain and followed JR to the bedroom and placed her on the bed. Eddie told JR about the fallen tree and that he had been trying to get her to the hospital. JR picked up the phone, but there was no service. Thank heavens for cell phones. JR called the hospital and told them about Devon, relaying the question to them through Eddie. They were sending the EMTs, and JR cautioned them about the downed tree and that they would have to take the back way in. Meanwhile, Devon kept crying and saying the baby was coming and it was coming now. Eddie and JR looked to each other.

"Isn't this when you're supposed to boil water or something?" asked Eddie.

"You do what you got to do, Eddie my boy. Haven't you learned that yet?" said a much-concerned JR, who finally decided that they needed to be ready in case she was right and the baby was indeed coming. There was no generator as a backup system at the big house, so JR told the housekeeper to find every flashlight and candle she could and bring them to the bedroom. JR found a scissor and string and grabbed as many towels he could find in the linen closet. With Eddie having worked in the animal sanctuary for months now and seen puppies and kittens born and JR's experience with his father's horses, both men had a little knowledge of what was about to happen, but neither had ever participated in a human birth. Devon was made as comfortable as they could make her. She screamed for Eddie, and he knelt down to hold her hand, kiss her cheek, and tried to comfort her. She told him something was wrong that the baby wasn't due for another five weeks. Eddie could do nothing to calm her. He asked JR what he should do. JR told him he would have to take a look and see if the baby was coming. Eddie took the scissors and cut away Devon's panties and tried to get a look with the flashlight. The baby was indeed coming. JR called the hospital and told them that he didn't think they would have time for the ambulance to get there, and that the baby was coming now, and they needed someone to walk them through the delivery. Eddie was shaking but looked to JR to keep him calm. JR kept reassuring him that he could do this; this was his baby and his wife, and they were counting on him. JR relayed instructions to Eddie from the doctor on the other end. Mrs. Davis, the housekeeper, brought a washcloth and cool water to place on Devon's forehead and tried to assure her that everything would be all right.

Following the doctor's instructions, Eddie positioned himself and got the things he would need close by. Devon was already exhausted, and the hardest part wasn't here yet. Her contractions increased in both time and duration. Eddie could see the baby's head crowning. Following the doctor's instructions, Eddie told Devon when to push and push hard then relax then push again. The head was out, and with one last push from Devon, his son was born. He wiped out the mouth and nose as well as he could, but the baby was quiet. Devon was in tears, thinking her baby was born dead. Eddie said he could feel life in it, but it was still quiet. Mrs. Davis took the baby, held him upside down, and gave him a small tap on his backside, and he began to cry. Eddie followed the instructions for the cord, wrapped the baby, and placed him on Devon's belly, all the while silently praying that the emergency squad would get there soon. With all eyes focused on the baby, no one noticed the bright red blood that was soon filling the sheet. JR couldn't move. He saw the whiteness of Devon's skin and feared the worst. Eddie saw the horrified look on JR's face and finally saw the blood. Eddie screamed to JR to tell the doctor what was happening, and JR relayed the message that he thought Devon was hemorrhaging. Eddie packed some towels in Devon as far as he could and prayed.

His prayers were answered as the medics came through the door to take over. Mother and son were rushed into the ambulance, leaving Eddie and JR just watching. Eddie tried to go with them, but he couldn't. JR told Eddie to wash his hands while he got out the truck. Eddie jumped into the truck, and they caught up with the ambulance as it was turning the corner, heading to the hospital. The ambulance pulled into the emergency entrance, but JR had to park elsewhere. Devon disappeared down the hall, and Eddie and JR had to wait until the doctor came out. Meanwhile, Eddie took care of the paperwork that hospitals ran on. Most of the information he couldn't remember but then remembered he had all that insurance information in his wallet. With the admitting nurse happy, Eddie joined JR in the waiting room. JR was pacing one way and Eddie the other; five minutes, ten minutes, fifteen minutes, both men looked at each other, and the strain was evident on their faces.

Finally, after a very long forty minutes, the doctor came out and told Eddie that Devon would be all right, and that she was brought to the hospital just in time. She had begun to hemorrhage and had to be given blood; she was very weak but was out of danger. Eddie asked about the baby, and the doctor congratulated him on a fine baby boy; everything was there, he said, ten fingers and toes and the loudest set of lungs he ever heard. He could see Devon but just for a minute. She went through a lot and needed her rest. Eddie saw Devon, who was groggy from the drugs they gave her. He told her he loved her and that their baby boy was doing fine.

Devon smiled, whispered I love you, then fell asleep. Eddie asked where he could see his son and was directed to the nursery. He walked over to the nursery, and wrapped in a blue blanket with a cap on his head was his son. A little sign in front of the bassinette said Baby Griffin. Eddie was beside himself with happiness; his wife and son had made it through the most harrowing experience and came through it magnificently. Eddie wanted to yell as loud as he could that he had a son, but he didn't. Instead, he walked back to the waiting room where he found JR still pacing. JR watched Eddie's face, hoping for some information. As Eddie got closer to JR, he smiled and hugged JR, telling him that the mother and son were doing fine. JR couldn't hold back his relief and hugged Eddie too. Eddie put out his hand to JR and thanked him for everything. JR told him there was no thanks needed.

"You do what you got to do," he said.

"Ah," said Eddie, "that Ledger line again."

"Heard it before, have you?" replied JR.

"Once or twice," answered Eddie. "I know all about you and what you did for Devon, JR. She told me before we were married, and I want to thank you not just for tonight, but because of you, all her dreams have become a reality. You did a good thing, JR. We owe you."

"You don't owe me anything. You and Devon did the hard part. I understand that since the sanctuary opened, it's the talk of the town. Something about a man who fixes abused animals and gives them a reason to live," said JR.

"People exaggerate. All they need is a little love. The rest takes care of itself," answered Eddie.

"Well, it's still a great thing you're doing. Now I think you should call Devon's parents and tell them they have a new grandson," said JR.

"Wow, I almost forgot them. Warren will kill me," replied Eddie.

"I'm glad everything worked out all right, Eddie. Tell Devon I said a job well done," JR started to leave. Eddie caught up with him and asked him where he thought he was going. JR said he was going home, nothing more for him to do, but Eddie told him he didn't want him to go.

"Don't you want to see your godson?" said Eddie. JR looked puzzled but followed Eddie to the nursery. The baby boy was perfect and made by the love of two special people.

"I know there's a history between you and my wife, but my son will need a godfather, and unless Devon has a problem with that, I want you to be it," said Eddie, looking directly into JR's eyes. He could see JR's eyes begin to tear and didn't want to embarrass him, so he told him to stay put while he called Devon's parents. JR did cry. He cried for the useless life he led in the past. He cried for the baby that could have been his. He cried for the life that could have been his. He cried for the happiness Eddie and Devon shared. He cried for the pain his father put Devon's mother through, but he didn't cry long. Enough time had gone by, and JR had finally moved on. He no longer felt melancholy whenever he saw Devon in town. She was happy, and that, he could tell. He could be near her now and not feel tortured by the past. He moved on and into a direction he never imagined. A few months after his father died and he was running up to the big house to take care of this or that, and he decided to move into the house and rent out his bungalow. He familiarized himself with all the business of his father and began changing things. He needed little to live on, so he started choosing charities to donate to. The seat his father held on the hospital board of directors, he assumed, when the president asked him to take it over, plus he took his father's place on the school board until the next election was held. Managing money was a little harder than he expected, but he liked the work, and he was beginning to like himself. He could have lost his life in a bottle of bourbon, but he saw the strength Devon had, the strength she always had, and decided it was time for him to step up, stop feeling sorry for himself, and do some good with the Ledger name and money.

Devon's parents were surprised to find JR standing with Eddie when they got to the hospital, but when Eddie told them what happened and how he never would have done it without JR, the worry changed to relief. Warren put his hand out to him, and Carolyn hugged him, thanking him for all he had done for their family. JR was not used to receiving thanks for anything because he had never done an unselfish act for anyone. This was new, and it made him feel good.

The family made their way to the nursery to see the newest member of the family. Warren had secretly hoped for a boy, and here he was, all eight pounds and two ounces, lots of brown hair, and when he made what looked like a smile, a small dimple could barely be seen on his left cheek. They stopped to see Devon for a few minutes. They knew that she needed rest more than them right now. Everyone left except Eddie. He stayed with Devon, holding her hand. He had to be close to her, to know she was all right after almost losing her. Devon woke when they brought the baby in. Devon had tried to nurse their daughter but found it difficult, so she decided not to try with her son. As she was handed the baby, the nurse asked if they had a name picked out. Eddie realized that he never considered a name because they weren't sure what the sex would be. They had asked not to be told when she had her ultrasound. Eddie was surprised when Devon spoke up and said the baby was to be named Edward James Griffin Jr. Eddie beamed when the nurse told them it was a perfect selection because from what she could see, he looked just like his dad. Devon fed the bottle to the baby, and when she was done, she handed him to Eddie. His son, he would have to get used to that, then he thought about his father.

"I guess I had better call my folks and tell them they have a new grandson, Edward the third. That definitely has a nice ring to it. Did I tell you how much I love you and how you scared the life out of me?" said Eddie.

"Believe me, I wish it could have gone differently myself, and I love you too," replied Devon.

"Do you remember everything?" he asked.

"Yes, Eddie, I remember. I remember JR, if that's what you're referring to," said Devon.

"I don't know if I could have done everything without him, Devon. I was really terrified, but he kept me focused and helped me through the worst time. If it wasn't for him, well, I really rather not think of what could have happened. I said something to him in the waiting room that maybe I should have waited to discuss with you, but I was just so grateful and caught up in the moment," replied Eddie. "I asked him to be our son's godfather. I know it was just relief that you were both okay, and it just came out. When I realized what I said, I told him that it depended on you. I'm sorry, Devon. If it's not all right with you, he said he would understand. I'm really sorry."

"Eddie, you're lucky I love you. I haven't given any thought to him since I married you. He's barely a memory. I know how frightened you were about me and the baby, so I guess if you feel that strongly about it, then we should go with your choice. I don't expect my mother and father to like it that much, but we'll make it work somehow."

It did work. The baby was christened. JR was the godfather, and Eddie's baby sister was godmother. Everything went smoothly. Within three months, Devon was back to work in the flower shop full time, and Eddie tried to spend as much time at the animal sanctuary as he could. His heating and air-conditioning business was keeping him very busy. He had to hire additional men and get another van. He still limited himself in the business, just doing the estimates and planning out the jobs. The rest of the men did the actual work. Eddie was so much happier at the sanctuary, and now that they had many more animals, he had planned to stop working in the heating business altogether. He had a very qualified man who could do the estimating, Aaron Hartwell; the man who worked on his crew when he was in New York was doing a great job, and Eddie knew he could trust him to do everything. Eddie felt he could do more at the sanctuary. Everyone commented on how uncanny it was the way the animals reacted when Eddie was with them, not just dogs but horses also. Eddie, the city boy who had never touched a horse or a dog, was making miracles happen. Once Eddie worked with a dog and felt it was time for it to find a forever home, he worked hard to find him one. Every dog placed was a welcome member to the home. Some animals, however, would never be rehabilitated enough to be placed in a home. Years of abuse and neglect left some animals too unstable, and so these would spend the rest of their lives living happily at the sanctuary, getting all the love and attention Eddie could give them.

One day Devon brought the kids to have lunch with Eddie at the sanctuary; Eddie took his son to see some of the horses. Eddie Jr.

broke free from his father's hand and walked up to the nearest one and said something to the horse. With his father now beside him, the horse put his head down and allowed the small boy to pet him. Devon watched in amazement as her little boy showed no fear of the very large horse. Devon herself never went near some of the animals, but here was her five-year-old totally embracing this horse's head. At lunch, Devon asked her son what he said to the horse. Eddie Jr. said he told the horse that he was safe now and that he and his dad would always love him. Devon looked at Eddie with tears in her eyes; this little boy with so much love in his heart for every creature was just like his father. Devon was so proud of the work they had done, the shop, pet store, and especially the sanctuary. Devon's dream was always to have a sanctuary for poor, neglected animals, but little did she know just how important it would be to her family. Eddie was happier then she had ever seen him, and the children adored their father, preferring to be with him most times than her, especially Eddie Jr. Eddie always told them to dream and to dream big, not to let anyone ever tell them that their dreams were impossible, and telling them that it was their mother's dream that made it all possible.

Eddie Jr. celebrated each birthday with his godfather present; over the years, it was no longer stressful to Devon or her parents to have him there. JR explained how the apple and stone fruit farm was run and told the boy he would be happy if one day he would like to take over the management of the farm. Eddie Jr. always listened attentively, but when he turned eighteen, he announced he was going to college to become a veterinarian. He had a way with the animals, much like his father did, and that was the way he wanted to spend his life, working next to his dad.

Emma, their daughter, was already enrolled in college, pursuing an art career. She painted many of the animals at the sanctuary, and her father hung them on the walls of the offices. Many people commented on the artwork and even asked to buy them; Emma was that good. After four years in college, Emma moved to California to work and paint in an art gallery and eventually earned enough to buy it.

Eddie Jr. came back home and helped his father in the animal sanctuary when he could. His own practice expanded to include three other vets and support personnel. Both of Devon and Eddie's children worked hard and were successful. They both lived the way their mother and father taught them; have a dream, and with a little hard work, they could make it happen. The only time they could all get together was Christmas. Devon and Eddie; Emma and her family, which included her engineer husband and her three children; Eddie Jr. with his wife (another vet) and their twin boys, who already showed interest in becoming vets; Devon's parents; and JR. Sitting around the large table at the lodge, Devon looked at each of her family members with pride. This was the last time they would all be together. It seemed like only yesterday that she was scratched by a big dog named Beaver. There was a song from years back called "The Circle of Life." This was her circle, and now one member of the circle was gone.

She had been sitting in the park, having lunch and enjoying the sunshine when JR walked by. He looked far older than his years; his face weathered from time spent making sure the apples and stone fruit were picked on time. Even though he had a completely competent manager for the farm, he still liked to get among the trees and check the fruit. He said it got him away from his desk, where he spent most of his time managing the Ledger's many businesses. JR still sat on the board of the local hospital, plus the school and a few banks. He also managed the scholarships he had set up years ago for underprivileged children to go to college. JR managed the Ledger money but was nothing like his father. He was a man well respected by all who knew him. Devon liked to think she had something to do with his transformation; little did she know she had everything to do with it. Her family was his family, and that gave him the life he always longed for. He loved them all, and they loved him. As Devon watched him approach her, he seemed to be having difficulty walking. Devon made him sit down on the bench. She knew something was wrong. She asked him if he felt all right, and he just smiled and said he was fine and not to worry about him. Devon reminded him that he had been a part of her life since she was eight, so she had the right to worry.

"You do what you got to do, Devon," he said.

"Don't give me that crap after all these years, JR. Are you sure you're feeling all right?" she said.

"All's right with the world, my love. Best life I've ever had, thanks to you." That was the last words JR ever said. He collapsed in Devon's arms, and Devon felt the life leaving his body.

"You made us all proud, JR," whispered Devon as she kissed the gray hair on the head of the man who lay against her shoulder.

Devon and her entire family had a few words to say about JR and the way he touched their lives. Devon didn't cry for him. She laughed. That was what he always made her do. Devon had decided not to wear black to the funeral after all. Even though she was brought up believing you should, she knew JR would have said she looked terrible in black. He always liked to see her in green, the color of the leaves on the trees he loved so much. No one in her family wore black. Yes, they were burying him, but after that, there would be a celebration of life, a celebration of all the good things he had done, a celebration for all the people he helped, and a celebration of all the love he shared.

"You did good, JR. You did what you had to do, and you did it well," said Devon.

ABOUT THE AUTHOR

AFTER A PRETTY SEVERE car accident, she learned that writing masked the pain of having two spinal surgeries. Thirty days in a rehab hospital and she learned from a doctor that she was right. The brain cannot think of two things if you are concentrating hard enough. She spent eleven months to train her standard poodle to become a registered therapy dog so she could visit hospitals and nursing homes. The reward was wonderful. She did this for ten years until the poodle passed away. Then she needed to write more and more. She and her husband have been married for fifty years and have two sons and four granddaughters. Graduating from Ichabod Crane Central School in Columbia County and FIT in Manhattan shaped her into this person she is today. Writing is for her; it still takes the pain away as she goes through more procedures and tests. What does she do for herself? She writes and writes.

www.ingramcontent.com/pod-product-compliance
Lightning Source LLC
Chambersburg PA
CBHW031522120626
46545CB00005B/1960